"Adoption not only welcomes a lonely c
a beautiful picture of God's love for us. In I Call ...
examines adoption through the lens of Scripture, pointing adoptive parents
again and again to the truths of God's Word. Through this study, you'll find the
sufficiency of Christ to help you parent your child with His love and compassion."

—Jim Daly, president, Focus on the Family

"I Call You Mine weaves the breathtaking costs and life-giving joys that most
always come together in adoption. This is Scripture-soaked beauty."

—Jedd Medefind, president, Christian Alliance for Orphans

"I love this book! It's got it all . . . God's heart for the orphan, the plight of the
fatherless, God's big, big plan to adopt us all, and an invitation to the church
to lead the charge. Kim has hit a homerun with this book. It's a must-read for
every believer! Not everyone is called to adopt, but we are all called to do
something!"

—Terry Meeuwsen, cohost, The 700 Club, and founder, Orphan's Promise

"Adoption and caring for vulnerable children is a wonderful, difficult, beautiful,
agonizing, hopeful, overwhelming, encouraging, gospel-displaying charge
given to every Christ follower straight from the heart of God. In I Call You Mine,
Kim de Blecourt has gifted us with a walk through the Word of God that lifts our
spirits and helps us see our Father more clearly as we go. If you are answering
God's call to care for orphaned and vulnerable children, you need this book."

—Rick Morton, vice president of engagement, Lifeline Children's
Services, author, KnowOrphans and Orphanology

"On the opening page of her book, Kim de Blecourt reminds us of the truth
found in Isaiah 43:1: 'Fear not, for I have redeemed you; I have called you by
name, you are mine.' (ESV). Just as this verse contains vitally important truths,
so does the book I Call You Mine. What makes Kim's presentation so rich is
her weaving vital biblical themes into the call for reflection on God's adoption
of us and our adoption of the orphans of our world. Each page drips with
verses and stories from the Bible. I Call You Mine is a solid theological work."

—Bob Flint, president and teaching evangelist,
Life Through the Word Ministries

"Kim de Blecourt's heart for orphans and those in need of adoption shines throughout this book. She reminds us that as an adopted people, we must be an adopting people. Kim's words will encourage and challenge you to see and care for the orphans and foster children of the world."

—Russell Moore, president, Ethics and Religious Liberty
Commission of the Southern Baptist Convention

I Call You Mine meets a real need in the adoption community. It's not only a comprehensive Bible study that addresses the theology of adoption, but it also focuses on the complex issues families face throughout their adoption journey. This book would be a gift to any adoptive family and to those who wish to love them well."

—Jennifer Phillips, author of *Bringing Lucy Home*,
30 Days of Hope for Adoptive Parents, and coauthor of
Unhitching from the Crazy Train: Finding Rest in a World You Can't Control

"As a grandmother of adopted grandchildren, *I Call You Mine* resonates deeply with me. Adoption lies at the foundation of our intimate relationship with and confidence in our Heavenly Father. This study is a gift that relates precious truth and insight about the blessings of adoption on both a family level and a spiritual level. I highly recommend this book for adoptive families as well as anyone who has struggled to grasp God's love for them."

—Shelly Beach, multiple award-winning author of
*Love Letters from the Edge: Meditations for Those Struggling with
Brokenness, Trauma, and the Pain of Life*

"Kim's new study, *I Call You Mine*, brings the darker sides of adoption to light—the parts of adoption many people are afraid to talk about or would like to ignore. Loss, depression, and grief are just a few of the topics Kim writes about courageously and vulnerably. This study will no doubt help adoptive families wade through the trenches of adoption—before and after their children come home."

—Jennifer Jackson Linck, adoptive mom and author of *Bringing Home the
Missing Linck: A Journey of Faith to Family* and *Jackson Finds His Voice*

"Kim de Blecourt guides foster and adoptive parents, as careful gospel practitioners, through the story of Scripture to find hope-filled remedies for those courageous enough to minister from the frontlines to the fatherless. As a former foster parent, I found Kim's biblical insight timely and love-based blueprint refreshing. Thank you, Kim, for your labor of love; everyone involved in this wonderful journey of caring for children will benefit from your work!"

—Todd Trumble, MA, MDIV, US Navy Chaplain

"I reeled from shock when I discovered the secret to my conception and birth identity at forty-six years old. I was not adopted, but I also wasn't who I'd thought. Life turned upside down in an instant at the reading of my DNA results. I needed my heavenly Father more than ever. I'd read the Scriptures that say God is a father to the fatherless, but it became real in a whole new way. No matter your identity story, Kim de Blecourt's amazing study, *I Call You Mine*, will encourage, inspire, and strengthen you as it takes you deeper into our Father's heart and helps you fall into His loving arms."

—Anita Agers Brooks, award-winning author of *Getting Through What You Can't Get Over* and *Exceedingly: Stories, Skills, and Strategies for Unearthing Your Abundant Purpose*

"I could not offer a stronger recommendation of *I Call You Mine* for the Christian who wants to cultivate a deeper understanding of what God wants to accomplish in and through them and their family through the adoption process. Scripturally based, this topical study is practical, encouraging, and relevant. Many times in my role as a nationally recognized adoption advocate and father by adoption, I have come to the Scriptures to receive wisdom and perspective on adoption from my heavenly Father, but never have I seen such a consolidated, focused, and practical study of what it means to adopt or to be adopted."

—Chuck Johnson, president, National Council For Adoption

"If you're considering adoption or if you're an adoptive parent, *I Call You Mine* is a not-to-be-missed study. Kim de Blecourt has skillfully woven her own story and the powerful adoption journeys of others into every chapter of this well-written book. With wisdom, compassion, biblical knowledge, and a depth of hard-won experience, she will guide you through each step in the process of becoming a family. Whether you study this book on your own or in a small group, you'll learn valuable lessons that will give you spiritual insight and take-home value. This is a powerful resource."

—Carol Kent, speaker and author, *He Holds My Hand:*
Experiencing God's Presence and Protection

"Wow! What an incredible resource for the church! Kim intricately weaves together stories, Scripture, prayers, commentaries, and probing questions to guide us to a deeper and richer understanding of God's gracious gift of adoption and how everyone can participate in the wonders of adoption here on earth. Dive into this study and meditate on the truths found within."

—Philip Darke, coauthor of *In Pursuit of Orphan Excellence*, president of Providence World, and cohost of the Think Orphan podcast

"Kim de Blecourt has done a masterful job of inviting adoptive parents back into the Scriptures to rediscover the loving heart of their Abba Father. As the grandmother of a precious adopted grandson, I highly recommend this Bible study!"

—Becky Harling, international speaker, leadership coach, and author of *How To Listen So People Will Talk* and *Who Do You Say That I Am?*

"Through relatable stories, practical application, and first-hand insight, Kim de Blecourt delivers a perfect study for foster and adoptive parents that not only inspires and encourages but educates and gives valuable insight to readers. This is a valuable tool for parents on the foster, adoptive, and special needs parenting journey!"

—Mike Berry, author of *Confessions of an Adoptive Parent:*
Hope and Help from the Trenches of Foster Care and Adoption

I Call You Mine

EMBRACING GOD'S GIFT OF ADOPTION

Kim de Blecourt

NEW HOPE® PUBLISHERS

An imprint of Iron Stream Media
Birmingham, Alabama

New Hope® Publishers
5184 Caldwell Mill Rd.
St. 204-221
Hoover, AL 35244
NewHopePublishers.com
An imprint of Iron Stream Media

Library of Congress Cataloging-in-Publication Data.

Names: Blecourt, Kim de, author.
Title: I call you mine : embracing God's gift of adoption / Kim de Blecourt.
Description: First [edition].. | Birmingham: New Hope Publishers, 2019.
Identifiers: LCCN 2018012797 | ISBN 9781563092299 (permabind)
Subjects: LCSH: Adoptive parents—Religious life.—Textbooks. | Parent and
child—Religious aspects—Christianity—Biblical teaching—Textbooks. |
Adoption—Religious aspects—Christianity—Biblical teaching—Textbooks.
Classification: LCC BV4529.15 .B54 2018 | DDC 234—dc23 LC record available at
https://lccn.loc.gov/2018012797

ISBN-13: 978-1-56309-229-9

18 19 20 21 22 — 5 4 3 2 1

To my brothers and sisters around the world caring for the orphaned and vulnerable.

I see Christ in your efforts to fulfill our Father's mandate to care for the fatherless. I am humbled to walk beside you.

CONTENTS

Fear not, for I have redeemed you; I have called you by name, you are mine.

—Isaiah 43:1 ESV

WEEK 1

Adoption's Foundation

DAY I

It All Begins with Love

God shows his love for us in that while we were still sinners, Christ died for us.

—Romans 5:8 ESV

Adoption is wonderful and beautiful and the greatest blessing I have ever experienced. Adoption is also difficult and painful. Adoption is a beautiful picture of redemption.

—Katie J. Davis,
Kisses from Katie: A Story of Relentless Love and Redemption

THE SEARCH FOR LOVE

His name was Sasha, and he was three years old. He clung to the fingers of the middle-aged woman who walked him into the doctor's office that summer afternoon in Izmail, Ukraine. Our son's orphaned status was obvious. His shaved head, mismatched clothing, and downturned eyes pricked my heart. My first eye contact with him seemed to seal his fate to mine. He was ours, and I knew at that moment that my love for him was unconditional.

It was during the adoption of our son that God led me to understand my own adoption.

I was not an orphaned little one in need of earthly parents as Sasha was. I had parents—but I lacked embracing and feeling the loving arms of my heavenly Parent. For most of my life I had been rebellious. I served no one but myself. Although I had been raised in a Christian household, I was not a Christian. I felt ugly inside. I didn't love myself, let alone others. I needed a Parent to rescue me, to save me. To adopt me. Unconditionally. Forever.

I'm overwhelmed when I stop to *really* consider the mess I was before God adopted me. It wasn't just that I was headed toward an eternity without Him. I needed His loving care, guidance, and discipline in *this* life. Right here and right now. I needed to understand the goodness of healthy boundaries, the depth of unconditional love, and the safe feeling of completely belonging to a family who would never abandon me. I needed to grow up under the watchful eye of a Father who would teach me and keep me safe, who would continue to love me even when I made mistakes.

When God adopted me, when He made me His and took me in as a full and privileged member of His forever family, it changed my life, my perspective, and my potential in a way I never could have experienced apart from Him. And it was all because of His unquenchable and overpowering love for me.

Having experienced that kind of love from God, I was able to reach out and adopt and love a child who also needed to experience that kind of love. I wanted to give our child in an earthly way what God had given me: healthy boundaries, the depth of unconditional love, and the safe feeling of completely belonging to a family who would never abandon him. And most of all, I wanted to introduce our child to the God who loves unconditionally—and who loves far better and greater than I, as a parent, ever could.

I chose my son—just as God chose me. And just as He chose you. God finds us first—before we even realize our need for a Parent and for a family. The orphan doesn't select the parent. The parent chooses the orphan. That is how the family begins.

It's the same with us. We don't reach out in love for God first. He chose us. He loved us first. That is how we joined His family.

And it all began with love.

1. Before God adopted us, we were far from Him. Read the following passages and list what condition God found us in.

   Romans 5:6–8

   Ephesians 2:1–3

2. In what ways do you think adoption reflects the concept of redemptive love?

WHAT LOVE DOES FOR US

Think of someone you love: someone you love so much you would die for him or her.

Now think of the opposite: someone you do not care for, someone you cannot stand even to be in the same room with. Would you be as willing to die for this person? Would you be willing to sacrifice the life of your child for them?

Probably not. And yet God loved us when we were far from Him, when we hated him, rebelled against Him, ignored Him, and jeered at Him. As sinners, that is who we are. Before our redemption and adoption, we were His enemies. We were filthy with our sin. Yet He loved us. God loved us so much that He sacrificed His one and only Son so we might live as adopted children belonging to Him. Think about that for a moment. What if you were willing to sacrifice for your enemy? Would you also be able to then take in that enemy and make him or her a legal, rightful heir to everything you own? Would you be willing to love with abandon that person and make them part of your family—with all its rights and privileges? And yet God did that for you and for me.

It is purely in His love for us that we are saved and given a fresh start in a safe and loving family. Our love is merely a reflection of His love. Our love is not the origin of our salvation. Our redemption, our adoption, is made possible only through His love for us. His spirit fills our hearts with love in response to what He did for us—while we were far from Him.

What does that love do for us?

The Apostle John tells us:

This is how God showed his love among us: He sent his one and only Son into the world that we might live through him. This is love: not that we loved God, but that he loved us and sent his Son as an atoning sacrifice for our sins. Dear friends, since God so loved us, we also ought to love one another.

—1 John 4:9–11

5

John reasons with us to display this love. We are to show the love we have so undeservingly received, perhaps especially to those who have done nothing to deserve it. No wonder loving, caring for, and adopting the orphan is so close to God's heart for His followers. God adopted us, so therefore, we adopt others. Often, like those we adopt, the situations God found us in were anything but beautiful or safe or healthy. What a wonderful reminder of how far God has brought us.

   3. In Romans 8:38–39, Paul described God's love for us. Read the passage. Then using your own words, describe God's love for you.

   4. How is God's love for you described in each of the following verses?

   Psalm 100:5

   Ephesians 2:4–5

   1 John 4:8–9

HOW ADOPTION REFLECTS GOD'S LOVE

People from all walks of life adopt. Adoption is not limited to Christians. However, adoption often means something different to those who follow God.

My husband and I felt strongly led to adopt. We had discussed that option even before we discussed marriage. It was part of who we were as a couple. As we studied Scripture and sought to apply it, we knew adoption was part of God's calling on our lives, a reflection to that child and to the world of what God's saving work does.

We have shared our story with other adoptive families, and they with us. Others have experienced this same beautiful awakening to the similarities between redemption and adoption. It isn't new or unique, yet often the idea of human adoption reflecting our own spiritual redemption occurs to everyone as a sudden and beautiful revelation, a revelation all made possible by God's overwhelming love.

> The deepest and strongest foundation of adoption is located not in the act of humans adopting humans, but in God adopting humans.
>
> —John Piper, *Reclaiming Adoption: Missional Living through the Rediscovery of Abba Father*

5. Write out what spiritual adoption means to you as you consider God seeking, loving, and embracing you.

6. In what ways does understanding spiritual adoption change your perspective on adopting a child into your family?

SCRIPTURE MEMORIZATION FOR WEEK I

For I am sure that neither death nor life, nor angels nor rulers, nor things present nor things to come, nor powers, nor height nor depth, nor anything else in all creation, will be able to separate us from the love of God in Christ Jesus our Lord.

—Romans 8:38–39 ESV

PRAYER

Dear Father, You alone could save me from the condition You found me in. Thank You for Your great love, from which I can never be separated. Thank You for adopting me into Your family. Thank You for choosing me— and continuing to love and choose me. Thank You that I can respond to Your love by choosing and adopting others, who are near and dear to Your heart. In Jesus' name, amen.

DAY 2

Love throughout Adoption

See what great love the Father has lavished on us, that we should be called children of God! And that is what we are!

—1 John 3:1

Caring for orphans means, in a very real sense, joining them in their distress.

—Russell D. Moore, *Adopted for Life: The Priority of Adoption for Christian Families and Churches*

LOVE'S COMMITMENT

When Lorilee and her husband Doyle adopted their daughter, they flew to South Korea, met their daughter's foster parents, and learned about Korean culture. When they met her, their six-and-a-half-month-old girl had already formed a bond with her foster parents. Lorilee was grateful they had invested so much love in her daughter's early life, because she understood her daughter had healthy attachment development. However, they realized it might be difficult for their daughter when they took her home as their adopted child.

"We looked different, we spoke different, and we smelled different," Lorilee explained. "Add to that, we were taking her from the only parents she had ever known. We braced ourselves for her reaction." But they couldn't have imagined the intensity of their baby's response.

She cried and screamed nonstop. She cried herself to sleep for a short while, but then awoke, took one look at Lorilee, and began to scream again. "My heart broke for her," Lorilee said.

Lorilee did her best to soothe and comfort the new addition to their family. After an extremely long and sleepless night, Lorilee sat her baby on the tiny bathroom sink's edge, placed her child's tiny

9

feet in warm water, and stood behind her. "We gazed at each other through the sink's mirror." It would be easy after that crazy night to wonder what they had gotten themselves into. But as her baby looked intensely at her reflection, Lorilee realized they would make it. It would be a long haul, but Lorilee wasn't going to give up. "She had me. And I told her, 'It's you and me, girl.'"

The crying continued all the way home. At thirty thousand feet in the air, Lorilee thought about what being an adoptive parent meant. "I didn't adopt my daughter only through the good and easy times. That's when it struck me. This is just like God's rock-solid commitment to us."

God's love for us never fades—it doesn't go away when we fight and scream and wail against Him. He remains true to us.

1. Reread 1 John 3:1 from the beginning of today's study—or read it from another translation. As you contemplate the Apostle John's words, what thought immediately comes to your mind?

2. Was there ever a time when you wondered how God could remain faithful to you? What helped you remember God's character traits and commitment to you?

3. In what ways have you considered your commitment level to your adopted child in light of God's commitment to you?

4. Read the following passages and list how God's love for you is described in each verse.

Psalm 86:15

Zephaniah 3:17

1 John 4:7–8

LOVE'S FAITHFULNESS, CALM COUNSEL, AND PATIENCE

God is the perfect model of faithfulness for us. The Bible is filled with His qualities of love and commitment. They are also evident in our own lives. It can be difficult to hold ourselves to such holy standards, and we may wonder how in the world we can possibly show that kind of love and commitment to our children. But the Bible offers us a beautiful picture of one person who acted with that kind of strength, a person who can be our model.

We often think of the Book of Esther as strictly about the importance of fasting and trusting God in our acts of boldness. But it also shows adoptive parents a powerful role model for how to love and stay true to our children. Esther's cousin, Mordecai, is a great example of respecting the adopted child and guiding them through difficult times.

We meet Mordecai in chapter 2 and learn of his adoptive role in Esther's life. Though the details are scarce, we learn that Hadassah, also known as Esther, had neither mother nor father, and that Mordecai had taken her in as his own daughter (Esther 2:5–7). It's interesting that since there is no mention of Mordecai being married, he may have been a single, adoptive father.

Through Mordecai's role as adoptive father, we observe three ways he showed his love for Esther and for God.

First, Mordecai showed his love through his faithfulness to Esther. In chapter 2, we learn that Esther was taken to the king's eunuch, where she soon found favor. While Mordecai didn't prevent her from going to the palace, we learn in verse 11, "Every day he walked back and forth near the courtyard of the harem to find out how Esther was and what was happening to her." Esther was moved to the grandest place in town, and yet Mordecai loved and thought enough of Esther to walk to where she was staying, hoping to learn how she was. Mordecai surely had other things to do, yet the adoptive father in him had to check and make sure his girl was OK.

The second way Mordecai showed his love for Esther was in his calm counsel to her. When Mordecai learned of Haman's, the king's second in command, order to exterminate the Jewish people throughout the kingdom, he calmly counseled Esther. First, he explained the order to kill all Jews. Then he asked her to go before the king and beg for mercy on behalf of all Jews.

When Esther reminded him that anyone who went before the king without being summoned could be killed, rather than getting upset with her, Mordecai once again calmly counseled. He reminded Esther that God would find a way to save His people, with or without Esther. Then he encouraged her with his now-famous advice: "Who knows but that you have come to your royal position for such a time as this?" (Esther 4:14). Removing emotion while giving counsel, especially while parenting, is important to remember.

The third way Mordecai showed his love for Esther is through his patience. Mordecai waited for everything. Daily, he waited to hear how Esther was. He waited for Esther's responses. He waited to see how God would answer their prayers.

How often must we rely on patience only God can supply? From the moment we begin to think of adopting, our arms become strangely empty, and it is only through God's love that we find His inspired patience to endure. As we bring our children home, we must have patience in the adjustment period and through each new challenge. Patience provides time to remember our commitment and depth of love. It gives us the power to think and respond clearly and respectfully.

5. Read Esther 2:5—4:17. What strikes you about the adoptive relationship between Mordecai and Esther?

6. How else did Mordecai exemplify love to Esther?

7. Of the three traits we looked at with Mordecai—faithfulness, calm counsel, and patience—which do you struggle with the most? Why?

8. In what ways could you rely on God's help and strength to pursue that trait for your child's sake?

9. Read the passages below and describe the theme of each verse.

Esther 4:16

Galatians 6:9

Joshua 1:9

10. Why are these themes important for us to remember and embrace in our own parenting?

OUR POWER SOURCE

As parents, we have the incredible opportunity to show the love God has showed us and to influence those He has entrusted to us. Throughout the many phases of parenthood, maintaining a consistent front, regardless of the tremendous love we feel, is challenging. This is especially true during times of adolescent stress or when your beautiful child is screaming anything but loving words your way.

Adoptive parenting often requires amplified parenting skills. Mordecai modeled wonderful attributes directly relatable to adoptive parents today. By remaining committed to Esther's well-being, providing her calm counsel, and remaining exceedingly patient, together, God was able to use them *both* in a powerful way. That's the gift of love in adoption.

Adoption is a family idea, conceived in terms of love, and viewing God as father. In adoption, God takes us into his family and fellowship—he establishes us as his children and heirs. Closeness, affection and generosity are at the heart of the relationship.

—J. I. Packer, *Knowing God*

SCRIPTURE MEMORIZATION FOR WEEK 1

For I am sure that neither death nor life, nor angels nor rulers, nor things present nor things to come, nor powers, nor height nor depth, nor anything else in all creation, will be able to separate us from the love of God in Christ Jesus our Lord.

—Romans 8:38–39 ESV

PRAYER

Dear Father, thank You for Your loving faithfulness to me. Thank You for Your calm counsel through Your Holy Spirit and Your Word. Thank You for Your infinite patience. You are such a personal, loving Father. Help me remember Mordecai's example while I pursue loving and committed parenting. In Jesus' name, amen.

DAY 3
A Heart Like His

You were taught to be made new in your hearts, to become a new person. That new person is made to be like God—made to be truly good and holy.

—Ephesians 4:23–24 NCV

God wants you to be just like Jesus. He wants you to have a heart like his.

—Max Lucado, *A Heart Like Jesus*

I SEE YOU, FATHER

I was turning in a permission slip at the school office when our son's teacher asked, "Can I talk to you for a minute?" Simply hearing those words stirred up curiosity and anxiety.

"Your son made me cry today," she stated. *Uh oh*, I thought, *He must have been pretty bad to make his teacher cry.*

"One of the boys was sitting alone on the bench during recess. I watched your son stop what he was doing and go to him. Soon, he had his arm around his classmate's shoulders and the boy joined your son and his friends and they all played together." His teacher was obviously touched by what she had witnessed, and her eyes welled with tears again.

"I was so proud of him. I thought you might be too," she continued. "I just had to share that with you."

And that's how it happens. Unexpectedly. Surprisingly. Joyously. All the love you pour into your children comes back to you in a short conversation, a note, or a shared photo. I recognized my heavenly Father's fingerprints all over that moment.

My small boy from another land and language had never known family. He had adjusted poorly to orphanage life, even though he had been there since he was only one month old. His rough attitude at three had landed him in the five-year-old group at the home. At his tender age, he scuffled often with the other boys and knew how to throw a punch.

Yet through the prompting only God can give, our family, from the other side of the world, stumbled wide eyed through paperwork, fingerprinting, and repeated processing. And through our naive family, God poured into our little boy's heart, loved him, and changed his life forever.

And when that teacher told me my son had turned and shared love with another lonely little boy, I whispered to God, "I see You in that child we traveled around the world for. I see You, Father." That's when the love of God took on a deeper, personal meaning. And all I could do was pray, "Thank You for this child. Thank You for his tender heart and love for You. Give me, too, a heart just like Yours."

> I will give you a new heart and put a new spirit in you; I will remove from you your heart of stone and give you a heart of flesh.
>
> —Ezekiel 36:26

1. What does it mean to have a new heart?

2. When was a time you witnessed or learned about a compassionate, "out of character" deed your child performed?

3. How did it feel to recognize God's fingerprints on your child at that moment?

4. Read the passages below. For each verse, describe how God's love impacts us.

   John 13:34–35

   1 Corinthians 13:6–7

BECOMING A CHILD AFTER GOD'S OWN HEART

When I think of having a heart like God's, I can't help but think of King David. David repeatedly directed his heart toward God throughout his life. It seemed to be what got him through so many of life's difficulties.

Whenever something challenging would happen, David would admit it to God. For example, in Psalm 31, he said, "For I hear many whispering, 'Terror on every side!' They conspire against me and plot to take my life" (v. 13). But then he would restate his confidence in God, "But I trust in you, LORD; I say, 'You are my God'" (v. 14). David would then continue his request and/or praise of God (vv. 15–16).

While turning to God when in distress is a simple truth many of us learned in Sunday school, I've witnessed many adoptive parents (and all Christians!), rather than crying out to God, turn elsewhere for help. And I notice only because I've found it true too often in my own life.

There are so many resources available for adoptive families now that weren't available even a decade ago—books, blogs, and therapeutic help in person or online. Regardless of what I was dealing with, I found

I started to reach for our therapist's phone number first, only later to ask God for His help with the latest family need or development. Can you relate? When I read David's psalms, though, I realized one day that I hadn't been seeking a heart like God's. I humbly asked the Spirit to prompt me to take everything to God first concerning our adoptive family's needs.

God answered that prayer and gave me the yearning to be a child after His heart, to seek His thoughts and counsel and ways first. It has saved me and our family from much heartache and many mistakes.

5. How can we pursue a heart like His?

6. In what ways can you teach your adopted child to love with a heart like His?

7. Read the following passages. How does each encourage your new heart?

Psalm 28:7

Jeremiah 24:7

1 Peter 1:22

FAMILY RESEMBLANCE

"My goodness, you look just like your father," the woman said to my daughter.

"Yes, I know," my daughter replied, having heard that same pronouncement multiple times from multiple people.

I'm sure you've heard it before. A friend of mine even jokes that dogs tend to resemble their owners. But it's hard to deny that there is a resemblance that comes with being related to one another in a family. It even happens to adoptive families.

One of the things my husband and I hear is, "Your son looks like his mother, and your daughter looks like her father." We don't feel the need to explain or say, "That's funny . . . one of them is adopted." We simply say, "Thank you. We are a family." We acknowledge the resemblance, graciously accept it, and revel in the mystery of it.

That's what having a heart like His is about. When we become children of God, two changes happen. First, we go from being dead in our sin to being alive in Him (see Ephesians 2:4–5). Second, our hearts start to be transformed. Little by little, the Holy Spirit sculpts our hearts. No longer having a "heart of stone" but given a "heart of flesh," our hearts respond to the Spirit's leading and to be obedient to God (Ezekiel 36:26). The heart change continues through our walk in the Spirit, only to be perfected when we see Jesus face to face (1 John 3:2–3). More and more, we resemble our Brother Jesus and our Father God. We are family.

This is what our redemption, our adoption into God's family, is about: family resemblance. Because it is through that family resemblance that others will see God through us.

Our human adoption gives us the incredible chance to see God's love for us through His eyes . . . as the adopter. That is what so many adoptive families have discovered. The marvelous, God perspective. All because of His great love.

> Ultimately, God calls us to adopt for Him. It's His heart that
> beats and breaks for the orphan, the lost, and the lonely. And
> it is only because He calls us, equips us, and sustains us that

we are able to fulfill His purposes. And I believe He delights in transforming His children into the likeness of His Son along the way.

—Stefanie Hanen, "Why Does God Call People to Adopt?"
Show Hope blog

8. Write out how having a new heart has changed your life.

SCRIPTURE MEMORIZATION FOR WEEK I

For I am sure that neither death nor life, nor angels nor rulers, nor things present nor things to come, nor powers, nor height nor depth, nor anything else in all creation, will be able to separate us from the love of God in Christ Jesus our Lord.

—Romans 8:38–39 ESV

PRAYER

Dear Father, You alone are righteous and holy. You have modeled perfect love for me. You have changed my stone heart to a responsive heart. Continue to lead me to love as You do. Help me to resemble You as the perfect Parent, as I strive to love my children. In Jesus' name, amen.

DAY 4

Fierce Love

Set me as a seal upon your heart, as a seal upon your arm, for love is strong as death, jealousy is fierce as the grave.

—Song of Solomon 8:6 ESV

I'm not sure when I first realized that my love for my children was a fierce love. . . . Whatever event or time it came over me that this was not a quiet, comfortable, sit down by the fire love. Rather, it was a fierce love characterized by strong emotion and equally strong action.

—Marilyn Gardner, "Fierce Love,"
Communicating Across Boundaries blog

LOVE CAN BE FIERCE

Love can be described in many ways—romantic, sacrificial, patient, kind, giving. At one time or another, I have experienced each of those types. One type of love I never experienced, however, until I became an adoptive parent, was fierce love. As I've spoken with other adoptive parents, they've said the same.

Alison understands this kind of fierce love that swept over her and surprised her with its intensity. She and her husband Bryan knew their second adopted son had heart issues, similar to their first adopted son. However, this little boy had significant heart and lung issues far beyond their first son's complications. They knew going into the adoption that they didn't know how his health would progress.

"I began questioning if I could [physically] handle it. Then I began questioning whether our pursuing this adoption was right for us," she explained. "I continued to pray for God's will. I didn't know what to do. I simply continued in faith."

Later that year, when they flew to China to finally adopt their son, Alison was still unsure of their decision and of her abilities to be a good parent through this kind of challenge.

While walking down the street in a crowded Chinese city, Alison was shocked to hear a song in English. "As we listened, I discovered it was a song of faith. I couldn't believe we were hearing Josh Wilson's 'I Refuse' right there, just as I'd prayed for God to show me His desires."

When she heard the lyrics, "I can hear the least of these, crying out so desperately," she knew her prayer had been answered.

"We were to adopt this young boy," she said. "He was our son."

From that moment, gone was the anxiety and fear, replaced by a fierce love. "Love grows along with your biological children inside you," said Alison. "The love that came with our adopted children was sudden; it was fierce how much I suddenly loved them." So fierce she would do anything for that child, go anywhere, fight anyone, and give up anything. So fierce that she caught a glimpse of how God feels about us.

His love for us is fierce. So fierce He would do anything, go anywhere, fight anyone, and give up anything—including His only Son.

Our fiercest love for our children is only a minutia of God's fierce and inseparable love for us.

1. How does Song of Solomon 8:6 describe God's love for you?

2. As a parent, in what ways have you felt fierce love?

3. How do you show fierce love to your adopted child?

4. Read the following passages, and ask the Holy Spirit to bring to your mind a message. Write what you hear.

   Deuteronomy 7:9

   Isaiah 46:3–4

THE FIERCE LOVE OF JOCHEBED AND BITHIA

One of the first adoption stories ever recorded was of Moses being pulled from his floating basket. This adoption also contains the story of the fierce love of both his birth mother (Jochebed, his Hebrew birth mother) and his adoptive mother (Bithia, his Egyptian adoptive mother and daughter of the reigning Pharaoh).

At that time, Egypt's pharaoh ordered male infants to be killed upon birth in order to slow the growth of the Hebrew slave population (Exodus 1). In Exodus 2, we find Jochebed hiding her infant son for three months.

She must have been an attentive mother to cover his cries. But after three months, I imagine she could no longer conceal his cries and needs and manage her household, so she created a waterproof basket, placed her baby in it, and hid him among the reeds along the bank of the Nile. She posted her daughter, Miriam, nearby to watch out for him. Can you imagine this woman's desperation to save her son's life? Forced to conceal him in the Nile, among the crocodiles, snakes, and other animals who went to the banks to drink and bathe. That couldn't have been safe for her daughter either. It's enough to make this mother realize just how desperate the times were.

When the princess came along and discovered the basket with the innocent baby inside, quick-thinking Miriam offered to fetch a wet nurse to feed the infant. At this news, Jochebed's joy must have been bittersweet. She got more time with her son, but to save his life, she now had to act as a stranger—a wet nurse. Commentaries suggest that Moses remained in his birth family's house until he was at least two years old, when he was weaned. According to Egyptian culture, this period could have lasted until he was six years old when he would have been presented to Pharaoh's court and when his schooling would have begun. Regardless of the age when he was taken back to the princess, the mere thought of that separation breaks any parent's heart. Yet Jochebed's fierce love for her son enabled her, once again, to do the unthinkable.

I have also tried to imagine how Bithia presented Moses to her father. *"I went to the river to bathe today, Father, and it reminded me of years ago when I came upon a little Hebrew boy sleeping in a basket. He's been with his wet nurse for years now, but here he is. I realize you ordered all the boys to be killed but I saved this one, and he is my son. I need to introduce him to his teacher. See you at dinner."*

Bithia named him, made sure he had the best teachers, and no doubt dressed him in the finest Egyptian styles. Perhaps she found her father's law cruel. Perhaps the cries of a baby gripped her heart in such a way that she could not let him go. Whatever the reason, God's hand was clearly involved in it—just as God's hand is involved in countless other human adoptions. Regardless of how this unusual situation transpired, Bithia's love for Moses was a fierce love.

Both women exemplify three characteristics that define fierce love: they are assertive, intense, and determined with their love for their child. Their love fought against the cultural laws and they each took calculated risks to ensure this boy would be loved, cared for, and safe.

5. Read Exodus 1:22—2:10. What part of Moses's adoption stands out to you? Why?

6. In what ways did Moses's birth mother and adoptive mother exemplify their fierce love for him the most?

7. Read the following passages and describe how God portrays His fierce love for you.

   Psalm 90:14

   Isaiah 1:17

   James 5:13

THE FEAR/FIERCE CONNECTION

I am convinced that fierce love is a spiritual response to the most common human condition: fear.

"Fear not" or "Do not be afraid" is found more than 160 times throughout the Bible. Fear played a part in Jochebed's story—would her son survive and live, or would he be discovered and slaughtered? I'm sure fear gripped Bithia's heart a time or two as well, especially when she considered her father's law and the fact that, by adopting this Hebrew baby boy, she was rebelling against the leader of the land.

Fear, in the form of anxiety, gripped Alison's experience of adopting a child with heart and lung challenges. Fear was present throughout the adoption of my son when I had to fight to keep him from being returned to the orphanage because of a deceptive judicial system in a foreign country.

Yet what I love about all of these stories is the result: over and over God used fear and turned it into a fierce love for our children.

When fear grips your heart, as it often does in situations involving our children, recognize your human fear as an opportunity for God to supply you with enough love to conquer it. You cannot be separated from His endless love supply. Ask Him to replace all fear with the love only He can provide—an unrelenting, fierce love.

> Joy emanates from the abiding sense of God's fierce love for us.
>
> —Margaret Feinberg, *Fight Back with Joy: Celebrate More. Regret Less. Stare Down Your Greatest Fears.*

8. Have you seen God replace your fear with a fierce love? Describe the situation. What was the outcome?

SCRIPTURE MEMORIZATION FOR WEEK I

For I am sure that neither death nor life, nor angels nor rulers, nor things present nor things to come, nor powers, nor height nor depth, nor anything else in all creation, will be able to separate us from the love of God in Christ Jesus our Lord.

—Romans 8:38–39 ESV

PRAYER

Dear Father, thank You for Your fierce love. Thank You for replacing our fear with a love so intense, it is like a blazing fire and a mighty flame. May we love others with the kind of fierce love You inspire. In Jesus' name, amen.

DAY 5

The Orphan in All of Us

When the right time came, the time God decided on, he sent his Son, born of a woman, born as a Jew, to buy freedom for us who were slaves to the law so that he could adopt us as his very own sons.

—Galatians 4:4–5 TLB

If anybody understands God's ardor for his children, it's someone who has rescued an orphan from despair, for that is what God has done for us. God has adopted you. God sought you, found you, signed the papers, and took you home.

—Max Lucado, *The Great House of God: A Home for Your Heart*

AN UNOFFICIAL ADOPTION

Our adoption facilitator was furious after he received the call. His anger was obvious as he explained why the Special Department of Adoptions (SDA) of Ukraine had called us back to their offices.

"It turns out that Sasha, the little boy you are visiting for adoption, has an older sibling," he said.

I immediately looked to my husband.

"We had only thought of adopting one child," I said. "But . . ."

"Yes. We should pray about this," my husband Jahn said. "However, my first reaction is we should visit both of them."

The next morning, we met Sasha and decided to adopt him. Then, we met Svetlana. She was a beautiful sixteen-year-old young woman. She had recently graduated from high school and was ready to start her life.

Before she greeted us, and without emotion, she stated, "I do not wish to be adopted."

Svetlana was old enough to refuse our impending adoption offer, and she knew it. Before we could reply, she asked for a pen and paper to handwrite a letter of refusal. She knew to do that as well.

There was something about her that I respected. From the beginning, I wanted her to have a relationship with her brother after we adopted him. I feared she would never accept us. Would she accept him?

After she finished writing her letter of refusal, she quietly asked, "Have you met my little brother yet?"

"Yes, we have met Sasha," I said.

"I would like to meet him too," she said softly. "I would like that very much."

Her heart was open. I marveled at how God brought us together. Even if I didn't agree with her decision to refuse the chance of a forever family, I wondered if there could be a chance of a relationship without it being legal.

"Father, we have met Svetlana for a reason," I prayed. "I see this orphan before me, and I can't turn away, regardless of what she says now. I recognize the spirit she has; she reminds me of me. The big chip I had on my shoulder when You adopted me in Your family. Help me see what You would have us do. I don't understand why, but I want to accept this young woman as a daughter, if not legally, then as a child of my heart. I need You in this, God."

GOD'S LOVING CARE

1. Read Galatians 4:1–5. Which phrase of this passage most stands out to you? Why?

2. In what ways does the word *ardor* relate to God's feeling toward you?

29

3. How do the following verses describe God's loving care for the orphan?

Deuteronomy 10:18

Psalm 68:5

Hosea 14:3

LOVE ONE ANOTHER

The Bible tells us so many times to love one another that I wonder if we, as Christians today, have grown too accustomed to the whole love-one-another theme. I see two places in today's world where love is most evident, however. One is in God's relentless pursuit of me. The second is the love adoptive families have for their children. It seems to be an extra helping of compassion mixed in with a love for children. There is something special about it.

In Matthew 22, we find Jesus in conversations with Pharisees, Sadducees, and Herodians who were all asking their best questions, trying to get Jesus to say something inadvertently blasphemous. After a few unsuccessful attempts, they came up with a question they felt sure would stump Him:

What is the greatest commandment (vv. 34–40)? This was the most controversial question, and in their opinion, should have no answer because all of God's laws are important. Surely they had found a way to trip Jesus up.

> Jesus replied: "'Love the Lord your God with all your heart and with all your soul and with all your mind.' This is the first and greatest commandment. And the second is like it: 'Love your neighbor as yourself.' All the Law and the Prophets hang on these two commandments."

Completely loving God is understandable. It makes perfect sense. The love your neighbor thing, loving others more than oneself, however, took me a lot longer.

Despite the difficulties, I have witnessed this selfless love countless times in the world of adoption. I have witnessed the love, grace, and mercy bestowed by adoptive families for their children. They live out the concept of *love one another* daily.

I have often wondered what our world would be like if every family physically and spiritually experienced God through the ministry of adoption. There would be a lot less pain in the world. There would be a greater understanding of who God the Father is. Peace and grace would be much more common throughout culture and would become the subject of newscasts and campaigns. Can you imagine?

The concepts of Christianity, the gospel, and adoption are all captured by this undeserved and unrelenting love our heavenly Father has for us. Father, please help us to love more.

4. How do the following Scriptures describe our qualification to be called children of God?

   John 1:12

   Romans 8:14

   Galatians 3:26

FROM ORPHAN TO BELOVED CHILD

Orphaned children often arrive with a mental list of survival tactics and beliefs other orphans readily understand. It is a list that gradually fades as the orphan accepts his or her status shift from orphan to son or daughter. If written, the list might read something like this:

You must be strong.
You must trust no one.
You must take care of yourself.

You will never be loved.
You will never be close to anyone.
You will always be on the outside looking in.

Our children slowly learn they can trust us. We become part of their routine. When they ask for our help, we are there, with consistency and love.

Isn't it the same for us in our relationship with God? We gradually learn to rely on His strength. We slowly allow ourselves to trust Him and accept His loving care. We hesitantly and skeptically accept the fact that we are unconditionally loved, held close as an intimate part of His family, and are now looking now looking outwardly to an orphaned world.

Through this God-demonstrated love, we learn we are finally free from questioning where we belong. We are no longer lost, we are no longer afraid, we are no longer abandoned. In Him, we have found our forever home. We are orphans no longer.

> We are not fit for a place in God's family; the idea of His loving and exalting us sinners as He loves and has exalted the Lord Jesus sounds ludicrous and wild—yet that, and nothing less than that, is what our adoption means.
>
> —J. I. Packer, *Knowing God*

5. Remember a time when you were lost and/or abandoned. What emotions were similar to what an orphan may feel?

6. How did it feel when you were found?

7. In what ways does God find you when you need Him most?

8. Write a message of gratitude to God for your spiritual adoption into the divine family.

SCRIPTURE MEMORIZATION FOR WEEK I

For I am sure that neither death nor life, nor angels nor rulers, nor things present nor things to come, nor powers, nor height nor depth, nor anything else in all creation, will be able to separate us from the love of God in Christ Jesus our Lord.

—Romans 8:38–39 ESV

PRAYER

Dear Father, You have perfectly modeled the attributes of an adoptive parent. You took me from an orphaned and hopeless state and filled me with belonging and hope. As I seek to love and accept the child I have adopted, create in me a heart like Yours, open and loving. Help me to love as You love me. In Jesus' name, amen.

WEEK 2

Planning for Home

DAY 1
Have Courage

Be on your guard; stand firm in the faith; be courageous; be strong.

—1 Corinthians 16:13

Then I started really studying what the Scriptures say, and God showed me that it wasn't my job to do the heavy lifting. No. That was something that only He could do. It was my job to seek Him, to trust Him, and to stand on His Word.

—Chris Fabry, *War Room: Prayer Is a Powerful Weapon*

COURAGE DURING PRE-ADOPTION

There is a secret most adoptive parents know well, though we do not always recognize it up front or even speak it aloud. It is this simple fact: *The moment we decide to adopt, we realize our arms are painfully empty.*

It is a different ache from what we experience with pregnancy. Though we are eager to hold our unborn child, we want him or her to develop fully. We enjoy the anticipation and nesting for our newest family member. Oh, that we could hold on to that same anticipation and joy for our soon-to-be-adopted child.

Sadly, it is not always the case, as the waiting can be so difficult. Sometimes, the waiting starts even before there is decision to adopt. This was the case with Rick and Marie.

"God put a seed in my heart to adopt before he put it in my husband's heart," Marie told me. "It was four years before my husband felt God challenging him to take a leap of faith and follow a call to adopt. I knew both of us needed to be one in this journey. It was through prayer and a direct act of God in my husband's life that brought unity in our decision to adopt."

Rick agreed to attend an adoption meeting with Marie. But still, adoption was not a part of Rick's heart.

Then, a friend of Rick's with similar apprehensions to adopt asked Rick to go on a mission trip with him to Haiti. Rick gave an immediate yes, but later he changed his mind and called his friend to give him the news. That was when God literally and figuratively pressed on his heart to go.

Immediately after Rick hung up the phone, a strong and uneasy feeling overcame him. He was so physically uncomfortable, in fact, that he went into another room and closed the door while he wrestled with what was going on in his heart and mind. After about an hour, he called Marie and told her he thought he should go to Haiti.

Once Rick arrived at the orphanage in Haiti, his reasons for not adopting slowly vanished as he observed the children and their circumstances and compared it to his family's life. He decided he would like to share his life with another child. "God changed his heart and the course of our lives," Marie said.

Have courage and patience through all the waiting, Mom and Dad. Our God wants to pull you close. He waits for you to slow down between completing paperwork, pursuing notary signings, and dealing with overnight mailings. He longs to whisper in your ear between home study appointments, agency updates, and training sessions. He is waiting for you to go to Him with your impatience and anxiety so He can replace them with His quiet truths and everlasting love. He longs to show you, through His Word, how He has modeled this whole adoption thing for you. Run to Him now. Tell Him everything. He is waiting for you.

1. In his quote, what does Chris Fabry mean when he states, "It wasn't my job to do the heavy lifting"?

2. What was your greatest apprehension or fear when you started your adoption journey?

3. Find and read each of the following Scripture passages. Write out each verse. Place your favorite on your morning mirror or next to the sink, and pray it back to our heavenly Father throughout this study.

Psalm 9:10

Psalm 31:14

Psalm 56:3

Proverbs 3:5–6

Romans 15:13

COURAGE DURING THE ADOPTION PROCESS

Spiritual warfare, especially as it concerns doubt, is a common topic at our local adoptive parent meetings. Not during every meeting, but enough that I have noticed. As I have listened and considered my own experiences with spiritual warfare, I have come to the following conclusion: Satan hates losing his grip on humans but especially on children.

When God sends His followers to raise little ones out of misery, Satan seems to take it personally and reacts strongly. His attacks can begin the moment we decide to adopt. Yet God has promised we can fully depend upon His power to work in each situation, if we will only ask. Doubts do not need to be part of the adoption process.

When chatting with adoptive parent friends, I often ask how they work through the doubts they encounter. How do they find clear direction? Nearly unanimously they have answered: prayer.

Prayer was an important part of Rick and Marie's continued adoption journey, as well.

While Rick was on his mission trip to Haiti, he was drawn to a particular young boy who had a delightful personality, a contagious smile, and a competitive spirit. After the mission trip, Rick told Marie about the boy, but Marie asked him *not* to show her any photos of him. She wanted confirmation of their adoption to come from God. She wanted to travel to Haiti herself and be sure. They committed their adoption decision to prayer.

"I was filled with mixed emotions," Marie said. "I never thought we would adopt from another country when there are so many children in our own country who need homes." But even with her concerns, she did not want to deny what Rick had experienced or her long-term desire to adopt. They continued to pray.

About six months later, Marie traveled to Haiti on a mission trip to the same orphanage. When she arrived, one boy in particular sought her out. He often put his head on her shoulder or snuggled under her arm.

When she arrived home, Marie talked to Rick about the boy who sought her out. When she showed Rick the boy's photo, Rick was amazed. It was the same boy.

"There was no longer any doubt. God had orchestrated this situation to specifically adopt this boy into our family," Marie said. It was an answer to prayer.

In Acts 16:16–40, we read about an example of the spiritual warfare Paul and Silas faced. After being verbally attacked by a demon by way of the young woman it inhabited, Paul and Silas were beaten and jailed (after they freed the young woman from being possessed). While imprisoned, they began to pray and sing hymns. Their chains fell off, their personal jailer accepted salvation, and they were escorted from their inner jail cell by the magistrates themselves. Paul and Silas responded to being beaten and wrongfully imprisoned by praying aloud and singing! Can you imagine? I love the physicality of their faith.

Regardless of your adoption journey, you will eventually encounter times of spiritual warfare and perhaps even feelings of doubt or defeat. The sooner you counterattack with prayer, the sooner you can lay the burden at the feet of our heavenly Father. He carries it and battles for us. I have often asked myself why I struggled so long before giving my burden to Him. Have your prayer strategy ready for when spiritual attacks begin.

4. How has God answered prayer throughout your adoption journey?

5. Read Acts 16:16–40. What stands out to you from this passage?

6. Read the following passages and answer the accompanying questions.

   Ephesians 6:12: What do we struggle against?

   2 Timothy 3:12: If we believe in Jesus Christ, what will we be?

   John 16:33: Jesus asks us to have courage. Why?

COURAGE DURING POST-ADOPTION

As adoptive parents, we all look forward to having our newest family member home. Yet while we all dream of a smooth adoption homecoming, adding any new family member comes with adjustments. For some, the adjustments are minor and without much strife. For others, a new family member (or members) can bring trauma, grief, and heartache.

These hurting children bring a host of pain with them—and as they come into our homes, the pain doesn't simply disappear.

Adoption is a ministry, and ministry often provides healing. A short life of constant pain, neglect, and abuse needs what we bring: the power of a loving, healing God. We are that connection for these beautiful but hurting children. What a privilege. A privilege that takes courage, because before we can experience healing, we must work through the pain of their brokenness.

Prayer is a powerful weapon. Encourage others to join your family in prayer once your family is all together. Even once the adoption process is complete, your need for prayer will remain strong. Prayer is a wonderful way to build support for your new family.

> 7. List the people who can be part of your post-adoption support. How can you best communicate with them?

SCRIPTURE MEMORIZATION FOR WEEK 2

Whatever you have learned or received or heard from me, or seen in me—put it into practice. And the God of peace will be with you.
—Philippians 4:9

PRAYER

Dear Father, how I long for You to be the largest part of our journey into the ministry of adoption. When I am filled with apprehension and fear, calm my heart and mind. Give me the courage to always answer yes to You. In Jesus' name, amen.

DAY 2
Understanding Trauma

Your eyes saw my unformed body; all the days ordained for me were written in your book before one of them came to be.

—Psalm 139:16

Adoption is not the call to have a perfect, rosy family. It is the call to give love, mercy, and patience.

—Hope for Orphans ministry

YOUR CHILD'S STORY

Our son was four years old when he joined our family. He knew he was adopted. We had no decision to make about whether to talk about his adoption. It happened naturally and almost daily. It didn't take long before he started asking questions about his birth family. However, I was able to provide him little information.

I offered what I thought to be true. Truth is always important when speaking with our children. When it comes to an adopted child's story, how and what you share with them is especially important for building your relationship with them. Trust is crucial.

All I knew were generalities. No details. It left an openness. Over the years, I have asked our son to fill in the details he seemed so desperate to possess. It was hard for him at first, but over time, these conversations became easier. I remember the day we got out all the documents involved in his adoption. We carefully went through each one.

He loved seeing his Ukraine birth certificate written in Russian. I had even obtained a small card that recorded his Orthodox infant baptism. He loved the gold edges and ornateness of it. But the most important piece was the small copy of his birth mother's passport with her photo.

He stared at her photo for a long time, as I sat next to him and waited.

"She doesn't look like I thought she would," he finally stated.

"She was young in that photo but perhaps older when she passed away," I said.

"I don't know how you were able to get this for me, but I'm glad you did," he said.

"I am too."

It was a sober yet fulfilling time of reflection for both of us. Whenever he asked me a question I didn't know the answer to, I told him I didn't know. I would then ask him what he thought the answer to his question was. Many times, he had an answer ready. Other times, there was simply no answer to be found. We learned to leave those unanswered questions in peace.

After we carefully placed everything back in their folder, our son seemed satisfied. I told him we could review these things any time he wanted to. He has yet to ask to see them again. I told him once again how happy I was that God arranged for him to join our family. He said he was glad too.

The entire scenario brings to mind the role anxiety can play in adoption, for both the child and the parent. He was anxious over the unknown. I knew the day of questions about his life before meeting us would come, and I prayed I would be prepared.

> Do not be anxious about anything, but in every situation, by prayer and petition, with thanksgiving, present your requests to God.
>
> —Philippians 4:6

1. Is there a part of your adopted child's story that leaves you feeling anxious? What part?

2. How can/did you prepare for the conversation regarding your child's story?

3. Read each Scripture and answer how it encourages you to address anxiety and worry.

Matthew 6:25–34

Matthew 11:28–30

1 Peter 5:6–8

IMPACT OF TRAUMA

As parents, we recognize the great privilege we have been given to raise our children. We also recognize some children will join our family who have traumatic backgrounds. How does the Bible speak to us about people living with trauma?

The moment I began contemplating this question, I was struck with the response: The Bible is full of stories of traumatized people. Adam and Eve after they were thrown out of the Garden of Eden; Cain after he killed his brother, Abel; Noah and his family, after he witnessed the death of *everything* because of the flood. And that's just a taste from the first eight chapters of the first book in the Bible!

While many Bible stories show us people who were traumatized, one story in particular illustrates three important things to remember when it comes to trauma. We find this story in Genesis 37—50.

Joseph was a young man who had almost a dozen brothers, but he was his father's favorite because his father dearly loved his mother, Rachel (the other brothers' mother was Leah). Joseph was pampered and grew up feeling entitled—he was spoiled. Finally, the brothers had enough of listening to Joseph's bravado, so they hatched a plan in which they would throw him into a deep well and then sell him to some slave traders who would take him far, far away. It's a terrible story, really. But we have some relatable lessons we can remember as we parent our adopted children.

Trauma is often a part of life.

In Genesis 37, we read about Joseph's demise. It is hard to imagine being thrown into a pit, let alone consider the horror of my family wishing to profit from me in this way. Even throughout his servitude, Genesis 39:2 tells us that God was with Joseph and that he prospered, in spite of his brothers' plans.

Most of our biblical heroes lived a life marked by trauma. No one escapes pain because we live in a fallen world. Although God never desired our lives to be so apart from him, He created a way for us to access him and to experience the true healing only He can provide.

God often works through those who have been traumatized.

After a false accusation (Genesis 39:6–20), we find Joseph in prison. Even there, God is with him, and in everything Joseph does, he prospers (Genesis 39:20—41:40). In Genesis 41:1, we are told a full two years had passed since Joseph interpreted a former prisoner's dream and that prisoner agreed to remember Joseph and speak on his behalf to the Pharaoh. Two years! We are left to imagine what those days were like, yet God was with Joseph. God's plan wasn't waylaid because of what happened to Joseph or the trauma he experienced. Instead God used it to further His plans for Joseph and for the world.

God works on an infinite timetable.

We often measure time bound only by our earthly birth and death. Only God works through our trauma infinitely and can affect all those who come after. In Genesis 46, Joseph, as ruler of Egypt, is reunited with his entire family. God has enabled Joseph to save his family from famine. From Joseph's family, though generations later, Jesus will be born.

Praise God that trauma is often discussed now in adoption circles. Many books, videos, and support groups focus on trauma and the adopted child. However, in our struggle to help our children, may we always be reminded of the role trauma played throughout the Bible and how God worked through it to His ultimate glory.

4. How is God's timetable different from ours?

5. In what ways do we or society expect our adopted children to be grateful?

6. Read the Scriptures below and write how each references a promise to those who follow God.

   Psalm 91:4–6

   Lamentations 3:21–23

THEIR TRAUMA, OUR TRAUMA

Conversations among adoptive parents often center on the trauma their adopted child has faced and how they, as a family, are learning to help them through the many phases treatment can entail. These are good, God-filled discussions.

Trauma also surfaces in another way. These are the tear-filled confessions of an adoptive parent who has just come to realize that he or she is remembering past traumas in their own lives that have come to light during their adoption journey.

Our trauma sneaks through when our guard is down, and we hear our parents' words coming out of our own mouths. Remember those hurtful things we promised we would never say to our children? But along come those sleep-deprived days, and they slip through our safety-net lips, causing tears from all involved.

Our triggers become apparent as we reenter childhood with our children. Ugly emotions often resurface. Recognizing our triggers and ensuring our children don't suffer from them or that we don't withdraw from our children because of them becomes a full-time job.

We cannot change what has happened to us or to our children. We cannot restore lives on our own. However, we know a God who can. Together with Him, we can make a difference in the lives of others.

> Adoption loss is the only trauma in the world where the victims are expected by the whole of society to be grateful.
>
> —The Reverend Keith C. Griffith, MB

7. Has God revealed any of your own trauma/brokenness to you through your adoption journey? How and to what realization?

SCRIPTURE MEMORIZATION FOR WEEK 2

Whatever you have learned or received or heard from me, or seen in me—put it into practice. And the God of peace will be with you.

—Philippians 4:9

PRAYER

Dear Father, You are our Creator. You are our Healer. You have provided many avenues of healing for us. Draw us close, and heal the pain of my children and of my own heart. Help us to become more like You. In Jesus' name, amen.

DAY 3

When It's Hard to Smile

We have this treasure in jars of clay to show that this all-surpassing power is from God and not from us. We are hard pressed on every side, but not crushed; perplexed, but not in despair; persecuted but not abandoned; struck down, but not destroyed.

—2 Corinthians 4:7–9

Since God intends to make you like Jesus, he will take you through the same experiences Jesus went through. That includes loneliness, temptation, stress, criticism, rejection, and many other problems.

—Rick Warren, *The Purpose Driven Life: What on Earth Am I Here For?*

EXPECTATIONS

Welcoming a new family member often presents new challenges and joys. Regardless of how someone joins the family—by birth, adoption, or marriage—everyone will have to make adjustments. Because the event is usually anticipated, we've already formed, consciously and unconsciously, certain expectations.

Reflect on what you thought your adoption would look like, early on, before all the classes, books, and conferences. Were your expectations a little romantic? I know mine were. I expected my new child to welcome our presence. Not the running-slowly-across-the-meadow-into-each-other's-open-arms scenario but a grateful appreciation of having a family, to be sure.

Those rosy thoughts of our adoption journey now cause me shame. I was so self-focused. I doubt I considered the fact that my joy was born out of his greatest pain and need. I had huge expectations, even though I didn't consciously realize it.

When I consider my unrealistic expectations, is it any wonder many of them (yes, I'm sure there were many) were unmet? I am convinced it is our unmet expectations that cause the most damage and create the most stress. Even the beauty of adoption can be warped and twisted by them.

The Bible is full of people finding themselves having the most stress-filled days of their lives. Jesus reminds us in Matthew 6:25–27 of what our earthly, daily life stress looks like, and just how empty it is.

> I tell you, do not worry about your life, what you will eat or drink; or about your body, what you will wear. Is not life more than food, and the body more than clothes? Look at the birds of the air; they do not sow or reap or store away in barns, and yet your heavenly Father feeds them. Are you not much more valuable than they? Can any one of you by worrying add a single hour to your life?

But how do I not stress over things going on inside my house?

The answer may lie in where we focus our attention and energy. Do we focus on life's craziness or on the One who walked on water? Do we wake up happy and find ourselves stressed by lunchtime, or did we die to ourselves yet again this morning and ask for the strength to focus on Him throughout the coming day?

It's amazing how focusing on Him keeps me calm. My mind stops spinning and becomes peaceful. Focusing on Him is the ultimate stress-buster. He meets our unmet expectations and calms them with His unrelenting love.

1. Reread 2 Corinthians 4:7–9. Personalize the message to your current situation, and restate the passage in your own words.

2. How can we avoid stress through prayer?

3. How do the following Scripture passages apply to stressful days?

   Isaiah 41:10

   2 Corinthians 9:8

   Hebrews 13:5

   1 Peter 5:7

WHY DO I FEEL SO STRESSED?

Stress is a personal thing. What stresses one person may not stress another. While unmet expectations play a role in stress, another factor can be God's love for us and the discipline He encourages us to grow under. How else can we strengthen our faith muscles and grow in our relationship with Him?

Our adoption was *not* typical. Our in-country adoption process took a little more than fifty weeks before completion. However, nothing stressed me more than when my daughter, already part of our family biologically, became ill.

Jacey was nine years old at the time. Due to the length of time the adoption took, after she and my husband visited us in Ukraine during Christmas, she stayed with me.

Stress of her illness overtook me. When she had trouble breathing at night, I couldn't sleep. Once her ear pain began, I couldn't eat. I was so filled with worry, I remember fearing my daughter might die. I prayed, "Not this, God. I can't trade my daughter's life for this adoption. Please don't ask me to."

The stores had recently reopened in Ukraine, after being closed for three weeks due to the H1N1 flu outbreak across Europe. I was able to locate a doctor, who diagnosed Jacey with a double ear infection and bronchitis. But it was the last thing the doctor said that pushed my stress over the top.

"We need to get this cleared up quickly, Kim," the doctor warned me. "Jacey's infection is the perfect, sticky environment for the H1N1 flu virus to take hold."

I believe health scares with our loved ones are the worst. We find Mary and Martha in such a stressful situation. Their brother Lazarus was very sick. They sent word to Jesus (John 11), who was in another town.

Jesus said, "This sickness will not end in death. No, it is for God's glory so that God's Son may be glorified through it" (v. 4).

Can you imagine Mary and Martha's stress? They had sent word to Jesus that Lazarus was very sick, yet Jesus didn't come. Then they watched their brother die. We know it was on their minds. It was the first thing they both said to Jesus when He finally arrived.

"'Lord,' Martha said to Jesus, 'if you had been here, my brother would not have died.'" But her faith was great, and she quickly followed with, "But I know that even now God will give you whatever you ask" (vv. 21–22).

It was the same with Mary. Verse 32 says, "When Mary reached the place where Jesus was and saw him, she fell at his feet and said, 'Lord, if you had been here, my brother would not have died.'"

Even after watching their brother die, their faith remained in their Messiah. Jesus wept with them for Lazarus (v. 35). That is amazing to me. Jesus took the time to actually weep with them. Then, Jesus performed His greatest miracle to date: He rose Lazarus from the dead (vv. 43–44). Their stress and grief turned instantly to joy.

Jacey and I made it through her treatment. God remained faithful, and my trust in Him grew. My stress did indeed turn to joy. We are blessed to have a God who never leaves us, who weeps with us, and who turns our stress to joy.

4. During times of stress, how do you like to reconnect with God?

5. How do Mary and Martha each exhibit their strong faith?

6. Read and reflect on each Scripture.

   James 1:2–3: Why should we be joyful when encountering trials?

   James 1:12: What is promised to those who persevere under trials?

   1 Peter 1:8–9: What is the end result of your faith?

FINDING PEACE

Where there are people, there is stress. This is especially true in parenting. Add unexpectedness to daily life, and it's easy to have stress overload. Yet Jesus invites us to sit at His feet. He says, *Look at Me. Keep your eyes on Me.*

It reminds me of a pheasant hunting trip I took with my father when I was young. Occasionally, I would carry the dead pheasants for my dad. It was a lot of walking for my short legs, but I loved being with my dad and our hunting dog.

The dog had run ahead, and the tall grass had become wet with mist from a small stream. There was a handmade plank crossing at one part of the stream. With the weight of the birds in the sack on my shoulder and slickness of my boots against the grass, I was not having any part of it.

My dad had already crossed the stream when he saw me standing on the other side. He looked frustrated at first. Then his face gave way to understanding. He crossed back over the plank and took my hand.

"Don't look down. Just look at me," he said, as he backed his way across the makeshift crossing.

That's what I think of when I imagine Jesus calling us to join Him at His feet. *Look at Me, child. Just look at Me. Everything else will fade away.*

> When a train goes through a tunnel and it gets dark, you don't throw away the ticket and jump off. You sit still and trust the engineer.
>
> —Corrie ten Boom

7. Think of a stressful time in your adoption journey. How did focusing on Jesus change the stress level for you? How will it change the way you address stress in the future?

SCRIPTURE MEMORIZATION FOR WEEK 2

Whatever you have learned or received or heard from me, or seen in me—put it into practice. And the God of peace will be with you.

—Philippians 4:9

PRAYER

Dear Father, thank You for my life, full of both stress and joy. May I keep my eyes focused on You through life's difficulties that seem beyond my ability to handle. May You always be glorified. In Jesus' name, amen.

DAY 4
Best Laid Plans

The LORD is good, a refuge in times of trouble. He cares for those who trust in him.

—Nahum 1:7

The biggest step in my healing process has been the willingness to be vulnerable and ask for help.

—Jenni Ramsey, "Getting Real About Post-Adoption Depression (Part 2)," *Lifesong for Orphans* blog

WHY AREN'T I HAPPY?

The day Jennifer and her husband John went to the hospital to pick up their soon-to-be-adopted son, the nurse warned Jennifer about something she wasn't expecting. The nurse told Jennifer she could experience a form of post-partum depression, even though she didn't give birth.

"I couldn't take her seriously," Jennifer told me. "We had been waiting for this child for years. Finally, our first child. *I* wouldn't feel like that. I had prayed for this child."

A week later, Jackson started crying—all the time. Jennifer had no idea how much sleep deprivation would affect her. She couldn't understand why her son wouldn't stop crying and began to wonder what she was doing wrong. The more sleep deprived she became, and the more her son cried, the worse she began to feel until she fell into a dark season.

"I wasn't getting in my Bible," she admitted. "I only prayed sentence prayers, such as, 'Please God, help him to calm down for just a bit.' It was only four or five months into our adoption before I realized I needed to talk with someone about this." She sought help from a local counselor.

The counselor took Jennifer back beyond the adoption. She asked Jennifer, "Have you given yourself a chance to grieve your infertility?"

Jennifer realized her depression wasn't only because of the adoption but because she and her husband had experienced a great deal of loss—infertility, the closing of an international adoption country's program from which they had wanted to adopt, and friendships along the way. She realized she had suffered through a lot of loss.

"Everyone is excited for your adoption," Jennifer said. "They host fundraisers for you. Then you get to adopt your child and bring him home, and it gets hard. And it seems like there is nobody around for you."

At the same time, Jennifer saw that adoption gave her a better sense of how God sees her. "I have been able to grasp God's grace because I am a mother to a child with special needs. I better understand, to my bones, that my child is fearfully and wonderfully made," she said.

When Jennifer started asking God, "Are You sure I can do this? Are You sure I'm supposed to be his mother?" God revealed how He wanted her to rely fully on him. Their son needs lots of grace. And she realized that is exactly the way God sees her. "I never understood the extent of God's grace until now," Jennifer shared, through tears. "The hard and holy work of motherhood happens behind closed doors."

Jennifer learned an important lesson through her experience: she should never be afraid to ask for help. "Don't be afraid of your adoption being hard," she said. "Realize the hard part is what happens after you get your child home. Our children have been entrusted to us. My biggest ministry is my son."

1. In what ways does Jennifer's story connect with your own adoption journey?

2. How is parenthood a ministry?

3. Read each Scripture listed. Record how it applies to your adoption journey.

Nahum 1:7

2 Timothy 1:14

Colossians 1:10–12 *The Message*

CHOOSING TO LOVE

It is amazing what we can encounter as adoptive parents. We can be prepared for possibilities, but how could we be truly prepared for what could come our way, except by leaning on God's strength and compassion? Many families have endured great trials while their child heals. They exemplify grace and patience nearly every minute of every day. I see God in them, actively being lived out. Their faith reminds me of one of my favorite sections of the New Testament.

4. Read Hebrews 10:36—12:3.

In Hebrews 10:36, the writer encourages us to persevere through trials. Then he reminds us of all who have persevered before us. Beginning in verse 4 with Abel through verse 31 with Rahab, the writer lists people of faith we can look to during trials of our own. Then in verses 32 through 38 he describes groups of people who sacrificed for the faith; they exchanged their norm for the better way God had in store for them.

By the time we reach chapter 12, we read about the cloud of witnesses we have to draw strength from. The chapter culminates in equating our perseverance to a race. The running part really drives it home for me.

I've never been a runner. Even as a skinny, active child, allergies and asthma always interfered. I tried to run, but without the proper oxygen,

I simply couldn't get far. Any race for me has always best been met by a slow jog, then walking.

But in the race of faith, speed is not a prerequisite. How we participate and finish is what God values. With the ultimate example in Hebrews 12:2–3 of Christ's sacrifice, the writer encouraged us to give our all to whatever test is put before us. By keeping our eyes focused on Jesus, it will help us not grow weary or lose heart.

How are we not to grow weary? Paul answered this in Galatians 5. Here he encouraged us to live by the *love* we gain through the spiritual realm. Feeling love may not always come, but Paul showed us that we can love through the Spirit's power by which He grows His fruit within us—one quality of which is love:

"The fruit of the Spirit is *love*, joy, peace, forbearance, kindness, goodness, faithfulness, gentleness and self-control" (Galatians 5:22–23, emphasis added).

We must daily make the (spiritual) choice to love, regardless of how we (physically) feel. Only the discipline of the Spirit can help us do this. Only our full commitment to God can make this possible. Only the daily dying to self—and only through the help of a loving and merciful God.

5. Do any of the trials mentioned in Hebrews 11 somehow connect with your own adoption journey?

6. What hard place did God find you in?

7. Read each of the following Scripture passages. Record how it applies to your adoption journey.

John 13:35

Ephesians 4:2

1 John 4:7

DAILY DOSES OF HEALING FROM A GREAT, BIG GOD

Our adoption journey came with Post-Traumatic Stress Disorder (PTSD) for me. After living so long in another country completing the adoption of our son, the separation from my husband and daughter, the fear of corrupt authorities, and the daily stress of living away from home all manifested into me needing treatment. My journey to healing would be one of the greatest lessons God had in store for me.

I first touched on this lesson back in Vacation Bible School (VBS) at my childhood church. We would file into the sanctuary every evening for one week every summer to see the day's total from our Scripture memorization competition. It was the girls versus the boys. And I was determined that the girls' team should win.

That's when I first memorized the Lord's Prayer. It had to be exact and include the reference of Matthew 6:9–13. Even though I memorized it then, it would take a lifetime of experiences for me to fully understand everything Jesus was teaching me in that prayer, especially the "give us today our daily bread" part, which became illuminated for me during my initial treatment and recovery.

God showed me how healing doesn't always come all at once but often comes in small, daily doses. During the healing process, new truths were revealed, and biblical promises become handles to grasp onto.

"Today I will go to the supermarket, even if I can only shop from the end of each grocery aisle, due to the stress too many choices cause."

"Today I didn't lose my temper as more household objects rode the porcelain express after being flushed by our new, sensory-deprived child."

"Today I finally understand the 'give us today our daily bread' part of the Lord's Prayer. I won't dwell on the past. I won't worry about the future. I'm just asking for the strength to get through today. It will only be with Your help, God. Only through You."

Isn't it just like our huge, adoptive Father to bring us healing in small, daily doses?

I haven't prayed "give us today our daily bread" the same since.

> Only Someone stronger than your greatest weaknesses, bigger than your worst failures, and brighter than your deepest darknesses could address the things you fear or regret.
>
> —Marshall Segal, "The Insanity of 'Self-Care,'"
> *Desiring God* blog

8. What has been one of your greatest struggles during your adoption journey? How did you meet God during it?

9. How does/would focusing on the "give us today our daily bread" part of the Lord's Prayer impact your day?

SCRIPTURE MEMORIZATION FOR WEEK 2

Whatever you have learned or received or heard from me, or seen in me—put it into practice. And the God of peace will be with you.

—Philippians 4:9

PRAYER

Dear Father, You are holy and wise. You know me. You see me in my brokenness. You help me see You more clearly through my relationship with my children. Help me remember to look for You, on a daily basis, in the little things. I love You, Father. In Jesus' name, amen.

DAY 5
You Are Not Alone

Do not fear, for I am with you; do not be dismayed, for I am your God. I will strengthen you and help you; I will uphold you with my righteous right hand.

—Isaiah 41:10

When we mother the broken, we meet the Father of the broken.

—Sara Hagerty, "When You Mother the Broken,"
The Better Mom blog

THE BURDEN OF LONELINESS

Adoption journeys are often filled with stress. However, adoptive parents need the most emotional support once the children are home. Along our adoption journeys, we have experienced many new emotions. We have been exposed to new cultures, within our own country or internationally. We have observed neglect, abuse, and suffering, directly or secondhand.

The experiences I found most unbearable in our adoption journey were the extreme loneliness and observing the profound neglect of orphaned children. How could I possibly explain all I had seen and experienced? When I first arrived back home, I was in no emotional state to be an educator regarding all I had endured, which meant all the things I'd experienced only brought on more loneliness.

Was I physically alone? No. Family, friends, and our church overwhelmed me with love. What I needed was someone I could pour my heart out to, without fear of judgment or condemnation.

That's when Dr. Joe approached me one Sunday after church. A retired missionary doctor, he placed his hands on my shoulders and asked me, "Are you all right?"

I was stunned.

"I feel so . . . so . . . alone," I said, confessing my feelings for the first time.

Dr. Joe nodded. "You may need to seek professional help, Kim. Missionaries often face a great deal of trauma. I recognize the look on your face. But one thing I want you to claim right now is this: you are not alone. You are never alone. God tells us He will never leave or forsake us. He will never leave or forsake you, Kim. Cling to His promise."

It was the same thing I would say to Jake's biological sister, Svetlana, months later.

As a family, we had been focusing on getting Jake acclimated to life in the United States. Through social media, I was able to keep in contact with Svetlana. We were helping her financially and encouraging her in her studies.

While we were in Ukraine together, Svetlana had a recurring cough. I was concerned and encouraged her to go to a doctor. She assured me it was only because she had started smoking at a young age. (You can imagine what I encouraged her to do after seeing a doctor.)

When she finally went to a doctor, she called to tell me that the doctor, whom she didn't trust, insisted she had tuberculosis. Svetlana was scared. She wanted a second opinion from someone she trusted. That required money *and* the influence of more than an orphan standing before those in charge at the good hospitals.

Svetlana needed to know she wasn't alone. She needed to know it, just as I had. It was then that Svetlana asked me to return to Ukraine. I could hear the pain, loneliness, and fear in her voice, and although I was thousands of miles away, I agreed to help her. But I also told her the words Dr. Joe had given me—that God is never far from us, He sees us and our fears, and He is willing to remove those fears and give us His strength. There is no condemnation (see Romans 8:1). There is no judgment. There is nothing but love in His eyes as we explain every detail to Him. All of our disappointments, failures, and times we just wanted to give up. Nothing shocks God. He knows we need to emotionally unload all that has built up inside. He has removed every barrier. Isn't that glorious? We can go directly to Him and just let it all spill out. He wants to carry that burden for us and replace it with His peace.

1. Read Isaiah 41:10 again.

   What are we not to do?

What will God do for us?

2. Looking back on your adoption journey, when did you first realize it was going to be an adventure?

3. Read each Scripture listed below. Record how it applies to your adoption journey.

Psalm 27:10

Proverbs 18:24

Matthew 28:20

SEEKING GOD

When I think of searching out God, I immediately think of King David and the Book of Psalms. Through his trials and temptations, failures and successes, he always returned to God. That resonates with me.

Throughout Psalms, we hear David sing of his love for God and how God saw him through the trials he faced (see Psalms 18; 25; and 121, among others). From the time David was a shepherd all the way through his reign as king of Israel, David knew his life was in God's hands and he could take all of his joys and sorrows to God, because God was trustworthy.

I love to read how David witnessed firsthand that God was with him. In Psalm 57, he told of being in the midst of lions and ravenous beasts. He recognized God's presence when God protected his flock from the bear and lion—something he then related to King Saul, which we read about in 1 Samuel 17:34–37.

Yet when I found myself needing to reconnect with God, it was a psalm written by Asaph, the Temple musician, who explained best what moved him from anxiety to praise.

In Psalm 77, the psalmist cried out to the Lord (see vv. 1–6). He explained he could not be comforted (v. 2) and could not sleep or speak (v. 4). Then he even questioned God, wondering if the Lord had rejected him (v. 7) and withheld his love and mercy (vv. 8–9). These are common themes throughout Psalms. Typically, the song would move from sharing the psalmist's ache to praising God for His love. However, in Psalm 77, Asaph actually shows us how we make that move from pain to praise—what that process looks like.

Asaph remembered what God did for him in the past (v. 10), he considered all God's works (verse 11), and he decided to meditate on all God had done for him (v. 12).

These verses offer us a wonderful solution to our anxiety, loneliness, and despair. It is the only psalm I could find to offer such a how-to section. And it led me to remember all the protection, grace, and peace God had always given me. Remembering brought me closer to Him. My closeness with God is what drives out loneliness.

In verses 13–20, Asaph does indeed turn to God's praises, as we should. It's a strange thing—even when my heart isn't fully healed or filled, when I start praising God, my empty, lonely heart becomes filled again.

Praise God.

Your ways, God, are holy. What god is as great as our God?

—Psalm 77:13

66

4. Describe a time during your adoption journey when you felt lonely.

5. Do you remember how God directly, or through someone else, lifted you out of your loneliness?

6. Read each Scripture listed below. Record how it applies to your adoption journey.

   Psalm 18:2

   Psalm 25:1

   Psalm 121:3–4

FINDING FRIENDSHIP WITH GOD

We live in a time where technology isolates as well as connects. We are blessed to have so many options where adoptive families can find like-minded support. Social media allows us to stay connected with friends. They can all be a refreshing reprieve.

Yet with all our technology, we are lonely. God knows this. He created us. He formed that place in our soul only He can fill.

Have you allowed yourself to become friends with God?

It is an important question to ask ourselves, especially during our loneliest times. God used my loneliness to draw me closer to Him. I have chosen to spend time with Him, get to know Him, and talk with Him. When I don't spend time with Him, I miss Him. He feels distant. And I yearn to reconnect.

During the lonely days of adoption, make sure to keep close the One who is always there for you.

> If there's a cause worth fighting for, it's this: children belong in families.
>
> —Nicole Skellenger, Orphan Care and Adoption Ministry,
> *MLJ Adoptions* blog

7. In what ways have you become friends with God? In what ways do you need to refocus and draw closer to Him in that friendship?

8. What keeps you from being closer to God and His friendship? Why is that? What one step can you take today to move closer to Him?

9. Reflect upon lonely times throughout your adoption process and afterward. Which one stands out to you? How did you find relief?

SCRIPTURE MEMORIZATION FOR WEEK 2

Whatever you have learned or received or heard from me, or seen in me—put it into practice. And the God of peace will be with you.

—Philippians 4:9

PRAYER

Dear Father, thank You for always being here with me. Even when I feel weak in my faith, You never leave me in my struggle. When I wander from Your side, please draw me close. I don't mean to stray. Call my heart back to You. In Jesus' name, amen.

WEEK 3

The Total Cost

DAY 1

Realizing the Cost

He went once for all into the Holy Place [the Holy of Holies of heaven, into the presence of God], and not through the blood of goats and calves, but through His own blood, having obtained *and* secured eternal redemption [that is, the salvation of all who personally believe in Him as Savior].

—Hebrews 9:12 AMP

Adoption took the Bible's most marvelous claim and made it touchable for me, literally. It turned abstract theology into a child's fingers and toes. Even the hard parts of adoption somehow helped carry both the beauty and costliness of the gospel from my head to my heart. . . . I'd long believed that God pursued and embraced us; now I *felt* it as eyelashes against my cheek and stirrings deep in the soul.

—Jedd Medefind, president of the
Christian Alliance for Orphans

THE TRUE COST

I am not sure when it happened. Perhaps it occurred during the adoption process itself or after we returned home. At some point during that time period, I finally realized it:

The real cost of adoption is not monetary.

During all the paperwork, form filing, and travel plans, I had been worrying about whether we had enough money. We had been able to pay cash as we progressed in our international adoption process—the application fees, the home study, and the US filing fees. We were count-ing on my husband's annual bonus for the rest. It should have covered the plane tickets and international lodging, the remaining payment to the adoption agency, and the in-country court and adoption fees. But . . .

It was 2008. My husband was a commercial builder, and it had been a rough year. In the thirty years he had worked for his company, he had always received a substantial bonus. Until that year. He didn't receive a lesser bonus; he received *no* bonus.

The money we thought we'd have to cover our expenses was now nonexistent, and it sent us scrambling. At first, we fought our disbelief. How could there be no bonus? Then we started questioning everything we'd done for the adoption process thus far. Did that loss of money mean something? Was this some sort of sign?

After wondering and worrying, we finally spent time asking God what it meant and what we needed to do about it—because we firmly believed God wanted us to adopt, especially since the Bible is clear on God's heart for the orphan (see Psalm 68:5–6). Finally, God settled our hearts and paved a way for us to borrow the rest of the funding necessary to com-plete our adoption.

All of those financial decisions were necessary. Money is an inevitable part of the process, and it was what I was most concerned about. Now, in hindsight, I wonder why I wasted so much energy on it.

The *true* cost of our adoption had nothing to do with money. The cost of adoption lies in the change of heart afterward. What I gave away was my comfort level with being comfortable. The sacrifice made was of my old self. Gone were the old ideas of what would bring happi-ness—career, money, vacation property. They no longer held my idea of joy. The cost of adoption for me was being willing to let all that go, and let this tiny, shaven-headed boy into my heart. Gone were the delu-sions that my family and I were going to adopt this child and everything would be easy and happily ever after. He—and all the orphaned children I encountered—were broken and in pain. They needed a happily ever after, but it could only come through a lot of healing, patience, and love, not money.

Our adoption taught me how to live out my faith. The money was the easy part. I needed to commit to the harder, messier parts, and that took faith. And somehow in the process, the adoption of our son humanized God's redemption of me. I could finally recognize what God had done for me and how much He loved me. I could understand the sacrifice.

Now as I parent and love my children, I have a constant reminder of God's love and patience for me. I am reminded of it each time I see my son's face.

1. Read Hebrews 9:12. What was the sacrifice for our redemption?

2. How do each of the following Scriptures describe redemption?

Romans 3:23–25

Ephesians 1:7

Colossians 1:13–14

HIS REDEMPTION AND OUR ADOPTION

Paul was one of the few biblical authors to write about our adoption into God's family. He took what he knew of Greco-Roman adoption (adoption of adult males to continue the family line) and expanded the meaning to include God's spiritual adoption of us.

In *Reclaiming Adoption: Missional Living through the Rediscovery of Abba Father*, Dan Cruver writes, "Paul knew something that much of the Church today seems unaware of—if we learn to first think vertically [God's adoption of sinners] about adoption, and only then horizontally [human adoption], we will enjoy deeper communication with the triune God *and* experience greater missional engagement with the pain and suffering of this world."

I came to adoption somewhat backwards. I had learned much more about human-to-human adoption before I had ever seriously contemplated my own spiritual adoption. I don't ever remember any of my

Sunday school teachers or church pastors teaching about our adoption by God. I heard a great deal about my redemption, the price being so dear—the very life of Jesus. I understood that part. But no one ever seemed to discuss the adoption part.

For us to be adopted by God, we first had to be redeemed, or bought back, much as a slave would be set free because someone had paid for his freedom. We were slaves to sin (Romans 6:20) and were doomed to an eternal death, the curse of sin. In Galatians 3:13 Paul wrote, "Christ redeemed us from the curse of the law by becoming a curse for us." Becoming a curse for us is called *propitiation* (see 1 John 2:2), which means to turn aside wrath. That was the price Jesus bore for us. He became our curse, then sacrificed His life for us (see John 1:17–18). That was the cost of our adoption. The beautiful part is that through Christ's payment, we are not only redeemed and found not guilty, God goes a step further and brings us into His own family, making us coheirs with Jesus (see Romans 8:17). I still find His love in paying this cost staggering.

Even now, years later, that recognition of my adoption still feels fresh. It took the (human) adoption of our son for me to finally understand the cost of my (spiritual) adoption. Christ's ransom payment for me enables me to experience all the privileges of being a daughter of God. I cannot help but praise Him.

3. When did you first recognize the cost of your spiritual adoption?

4. What three words would you use to explain the message of the New Testament?

5. How do the following Scriptures describe our *propitiation*?

Romans 3:25

1 John 2:2

1 John 4:10

ADOPTION AND OUR TRIUNE GOD

Each Person of our Triune God plays a role in our spiritual adoption. In week one of this study, we discussed how God's love for us described perfectly His role as the loving heavenly Father who pursued us through adoption (1 John 3:1). In today's study, we look at how Jesus Christ, the Son of God, redeemed us by becoming the curse we bore (see Galatians 3:13), but we also consider the Spirit of God, who allowed us to cry out to God the (adoptive) Father for our salvation (see Romans 8:15).

Our Triune God made our adoption possible. When we adopt a child or children, we, in essence, imitate what our heavenly Father has done for us. Yet even in our feeble imitation, eternal life is illuminated for not only the adopted, but for the adopters.

> Were I asked to focus the New Testament message in three words, my proposal would be *adoption through propitiation*, and I do not expect ever to meet a richer or more pregnant summary of the gospel than that.
>
> —J. I. Packer, *Knowing God*

6. How would you explain your spiritual adoption to others?

7. In what ways does it make you view your own life and parental role differently?

SCRIPTURE MEMORIZATION FOR WEEK 3

He did not enter by means of the blood of goats and calves; but he entered the Most Holy Place once for all by his own blood, thus obtaining eternal redemption.

—Hebrews 9:12

PRAYER

Dear Father, thank You for being such a personal God. You call us to the ministry of adoption because You have adopted us into Your family. You allow us to see You in this new way. Thank You for sending Your only Son to bear our cost, our curse. In Jesus' name, amen.

DAY 2

What Faith in Adoption Looks Like

Whoever takes the lowly position of this child is the greatest in the kingdom of heaven. And whoever welcomes one such child in my name welcomes me.

—Matthew 18:4–5

Faith does not operate in the realm of the possible. There is no glory for God in that which is humanly possible. Faith begins where man's power ends.

—George Müller

MY MISTAKES, HIS GRACE

As adoptive parents, we work hard to merge biological children and adopted children into one family. Our goal is to ensure that all *our* children are *all* our children—loved and blessed and honored equally. And we want our children to do the same—not to see one another as biological or adopted but all as children of the same family. Though we work to forget any differences, the reality is we must also always remember our adopted children came from backgrounds that aren't as easily forgotten. Trauma cannot be quickly swept away just because our adopted children now share our last name. They must heal, and often that healing takes time, patience, unconditional love, and a lot of tolerance.

In our case, for months after we brought our son Jake home to live with us, he suffered from nightmares. We decided it would be best for

Jake to get counseling to help him—and us—understand the roots of his trauma and to deal with it in a healthy way.

Dina and Stan understand this issue all too well. When they adopted two brothers through foster care, they were not prepared for the amount of trauma they would experience. And even though the boys are now in a safe environment, the reality of what they experienced and how that continues to influence them has proven very challenging to Dina and Stan's family. The boys continue to lash out at the family who is loving them now.

Dina and Stan know that while the short-term is difficult, they must keep focused on the long-term, so they forge ahead, blending their family into one, while continually explaining, loving, and supervising the boys' safety. This includes not holding the boys' lashing-out behavior against them.

"I still remember the day my daughter recognized how I purposely get up every day and deal with severe trauma-induced incidents, and yet show them love, even when our two young adopted sons are behaving in the most unlovable ways," Dina said. "I love them without any hope of their immediate love in return. Unconditional love is my ultimate goal for all of our children—whether biological or adopted."

As Dina reflected on her biological daughter's comment to her about witnessing Dina's efforts of unconditional love for their two newest family members, she experienced an aha moment. "That's the way God loves us. Even when we're our most unlovable, He still loves," she said. She recognizes how much she takes God for granted. "When I mess up, I recognize His mercy and grace more now. I can accept His mercy and grace easier. When I'm not very loveable, and I reflect on that later, I see God in the details. My mistakes, His grace. It's beautifully woven together."

Adoptive families can face hard days while children deal with the intense emotional reactions to their previous trauma or abuse—trauma that may raise its head at the most unlikely times and in the most unlikely places. Yet in the midst of facing that trauma, as believers we are not without hope or help. We can rest in God, for He protects us. As it says in Psalm 91:4–5 (CEV), "He will spread his wings over you and keep you secure. His faithfulness is like a shield or a city wall. You won't need to worry about dangers at night or arrows during the day." Even when we don't see it, we must remember that trauma *is* there, and we deal with it and our children as lovingly and as full of grace as we can. Just as God deals with us.

1. What aspect of adoption has challenged you most?

2. What have you learned from this challenge?

3. How do each of the following Scriptures describe helping others with burdens?

   Proverbs 3:27

   Romans 15:1

   Galatians 6:2

FAITH IN ACTION

I had the privilege of working with a fantastic organization, Food for Orphans. Their tagline is "Giving hope one meal at a time." Through indigenous Christian leaders, they provide meals to orphans who would otherwise go hungry in the world's most forsaken countries. Its founder,

Gary VanDyke, has a saying that describes his faith and his life's work: "What good is it if I fill their belly if they still go to hell?" Through Food for Orphans, Gary works hard to do both: fill their hungry bellies and hearts.

When I meet people like Gary and like Stan and Dina, their faith and actions remind me of James 2:14–17 (AMP).

> What is the benefit, my fellow believers, if someone claims to have faith but has no [good] works [as evidence]? Can that [kind of] faith save him? [No, a mere claim of faith is not sufficient— genuine faith produces good works.] If a brother or sister is without [adequate] clothing and lacks [enough] food for each day, and one of you says to them, "Go in peace [with my blessing], [keep] warm and feed yourselves," but he does not give them the necessities for the body, what good does that do? So too, faith, if it does not have works [to back it up], is by itself dead [inoperative and ineffective].

The point James was making is that our faith is dead if there isn't any action to demonstrate and authenticate it. Why else would someone get up each day to purposely help small children heal from their trauma and all that accompanies it? Why else would someone dedicate his life to feeding children from around the world he has never met?

Trauma, to whatever extent, in our children is often par for the course with adoption, so while we lean on God for strength, we must never give up fighting for our children to be whole and healthy, to see God at work in their—and our—lives, and to live out daily the calling God has placed on us as parents who have welcomed in the stranger and made him or her part of their home and family.

4. How has God best equipped you to authenticate your faith through action?

5. In each of the following Scripture passages, answer how faith is to be acted upon.

Psalm 119:60

Matthew 7:24

John 13:15–17

FAITH AND ADOPTION

Adoption is a beautiful expression of the gospel. While caring for the orphaned and vulnerable isn't done as a form of evangelism, sharing our faith is a natural outcome—both to our children and to a watching world. When we open our homes and hearts to orphans, we experience God's love for us and then get the amazing opportunity to show it to others—starting with our own families.

In the midst of the darkest, toughest days and nights, God sees what you do. He sees your desire to love unconditionally, to give wholeheartedly of your heart and life to a precious child who desperately needs safety and patience and healing. Even though you cannot see the outcome right now, as Dina knows, what you are doing makes a difference—especially on the tough days, the days when you feel you might be doing everything wrong. You are extending so much grace, and much grace will be extended to you in return. It is yours for the asking. As Jesus reminded us in Matthew 7:7, "Ask and it will be given to you; seek and you will find; knock and the door will be opened to you."

> Parents with the most challenging children need support. If the parents get too tired to provide nurture, children cannot do well. Parents have to go through a mental shift, recognizing that supporting people with special needs is a priority in society. It is appropriate and necessary to get support for the family when members have special needs.
>
> —Deborah D. Gray, *Attaching in Adoption: Practical Tools for Today's Parents*

83

6. How do you handle your rough days?

7. Is there a way to bring God into your rough days? What would that look like?

8. Reflect on the ways you've noticed your children's adoption journey being like that of your spiritual journey. Write your reflections below.

SCRIPTURE MEMORIZATION FOR WEEK 3

He did not enter by means of the blood of goats and calves; but he entered the Most Holy Place once for all by his own blood, thus obtaining eternal redemption.

—Hebrews 9:12

PRAYER

Dear Father, You have made Your love physical for me in the sacrifice of Your only Son. Living sacrificially does not come easy for me. It is only through Your strength that I can truly show Your love. Help me make my faith in You known by my actions. In Jesus' name, amen.

DAY 3

Losing and Keeping Friendships

A friend loves at all times, and a brother is born for a time of adversity.

—Proverbs 17:17

If your heart is stirred, as it often is after you have adopted, to serve struggling expectant moms, advocate for waiting children, or bring Christmas to an orphanage across the world, some may think you've lost it and are in need of some intervention to bring you back to "real life."

—*Kelly Raudenbush*, "Adoption. Friendships. What No One Prepped Me For," *My Over Thinking* blog

ADOPTION AND FRIENDSHIPS

There's something no one tells you about post-adoption friendships. I found out the hard way.

While preparing for our adoption, I was totally engrossed in the whole process. I read more books than required (that's nothing new for me). I researched the country we were adopting our child from (even though I had been there before). I even brushed up on the very little Russian I knew, since almost half of Ukraine speaks Russian, especially in the eastern and southern areas.

What I wasn't into was the care and feeding of my friends. Looking back, I can see that my friendships had started to decline before we adopted. I was married with a little girl whom we adored. Adding the adoption process to an already busy family and church life allowed me little time for coffee chats. I was in Adoption Mode (I know you understand).

After the adoption, when I really needed my friends, though, they were hard to find. It should have come as no surprise, since I'd neglected them and blown off their invitations to join them in their lives. But still, I was shocked by the number of friendships (even from within my extended family) I seemed to lose.

Regardless of when pre- and post-adoptive friendships begin to fray, you will be forced to face and sift through friendship frustrations, unmet expectations, or miscommunication issues. You will have to let some friends go, some friends will let *you* go, and you'll discover new friends along the way.

My friend Erin was a godsend. We were friends before I started the adoption journey, when all the paperwork and process became all-consuming, and she stuck with me through it all. When I would close off from her or cancel a get-together with her, she would contact me. She fought to retain our friendship and to stay in my life. I am sure I may have unintentionally hurt her feelings at times, but she never let it show. She let me know she was praying for me. She asked if I needed anything. She has remained a good friend.

If you have a friend whom you treasure and you find that friend starting to drift, take the effort to reconnect and hang on. Some friends are worth fighting for, even if the friendship ends up a little different from how it started. Why? Because we need friends. We need them emotionally and to help us transition through this time of adoption and resettlement. Even if they don't completely understand what you're going through or why, they can be a great source of encouragement, strength, and prayer. Hang on with both hands—especially those you can count on when things get tough—and remember to be in prayer about them the entire time. And when you lose friends, mourn that loss, consider what you could have done differently, if anything, and then move on.

Eventually a new normal will emerge. You will find surprising opportunities for new friendships. There is truly nothing like time with a good friend, old or new. But also know that losing a friend may be part of the cost of your adoption journey.

1. In what ways have you noticed your post-adoption friendships have changed? Why do you think that is?

2. Are there ways you can rekindle a friendship you let slide during the adoption process?

3. What is one step you can take today (or this week) to reconnect with that friend?

4. Read each Scripture and write how it describes an element of friendship.

Proverbs 27:17

Hebrews 10:24

1 Peter 4:8–10

THE DEDICATION OF A GODLY FRIEND

Friendships are so important in our lives. Fortunately, the Bible has much to say about the value of friendships. One friendship in particular shows the essence of a godly friend. Found in 1 and 2 Samuel, David and Jonathan's friendship is truly remarkable, given they should have been enemies, or at least, wary of each other. Their friendship, however, gives us a great model of three qualities we can seek when we're looking for friends to help us successfully live our life as an adoptive family.

The first quality is a *spiritual* friendship. In 1 Samuel 18:1 (*The Message*) we read, "By the time David had finished reporting to Saul, Jonathan was deeply impressed with David—an immediate bond was forged between them. He became totally committed to David. From that point on he would be David's number-one advocate and friend." Such an immediate bond could only have been forged by the Holy Spirit. David needed Jonathan in his life over the coming months, and God provided a loving friend in Jonathan. When a friend comes into our lives at just the right time, it is easy to recognize God working in the background. Such godly friends share a spiritual bond.

The second quality is a *loving* friendship. In 1 Samuel 18:3–4 (*The Message*) it says, "Jonathan, out of his deep love for David, made a covenant with him. He formalized it with solemn gifts: his own royal robe and weapons—armor, sword, bow, and belt." Immediately, Jonathan discerned that David was the God-appointed next king of Israel, even though Jonathan was traditionally considered next in line for that position, as King Saul's son. Jonathan physically showed David his commitment to him, as the next king, by giving him his royal robe and armor, essentially making David the next in line for the throne. Jonathan displayed nothing but love and respect for David as king. Such godly friends love the other person more than themselves. Those are the friendships we can cherish most and most desire to emulate.

The third quality is a *prioritizing* friendship. In 1 Samuel 23:16–18 (*The Message*) we read, "Jonathan, Saul's son, visited David at Horesh and encouraged him in God. He said, 'Don't despair. My father, Saul, can't lay a hand on you. You will be Israel's king and I'll be right at your side to help. And my father knows it.' Then the two of them made a covenant before GOD. David stayed at Horesh and Jonathan went home." While David was hiding from King Saul, because Saul was seeking to kill him out of fear and jealousy, Jonathan purposely sought David out to encourage him. Then he made a promise to David, assuring him that David would be the next king and Jonathan would be there at his side to help him in whatever way he could. Such godly friends are able to prioritize the other friend's needs above their own.

David recognized the value of Jonathan's friendship. In 2 Samuel 1:11–12, we read that David tore his clothing, wept, mourned, and fasted when he learned of Jonathan's (and Saul's) death. David remembered and honored Jonathan when he treated kindly Jonathan's remaining family and servants (see 2 Samuel 9).

A godly friend can have a lasting impact in our lives. My children and I pray about making godly friends. I pray to be found worthy of such friendship and determine to be that kind of friend back.

5. In what ways have friends been there for you during your adoption journey?

6. How has a friendship enhanced your Christian walk?

7. How has a godly friendship encouraged you in your day-to-day experience as an adoptive parent?

8. Read the following Scriptures. Describe the benefits of friendship you find in each.

Ecclesiastes 4:9–12

Romans 1:12

1 Thessalonians 5:11

LASTING FRIENDSHIPS

Our adoption journey has taught me the value of true and lasting friendships. Many wanted updates along our journey so they could know how to encourage and pray for us. My godly friends went above and beyond and asked how they could help (and wouldn't accept "nothing" as an answer), and then they followed through.

Encouragement was their gift to me. They would write the verses and send them to me. They prayed with me. While I was living in Ukraine, they took meals to our house, provided afterschool care for our daughter, and kept me informed of events from home. Their thoughtfulness meant so much.

God places friends in our lives at the right moment. Although the reality of life with a newly-adopted child may mean you must let some friends go, you can rest assured that God will provide friends who do understand and value this important season in your family's life. Valuing our friendships is an important, time-worthy activity. It is a form of self-care you will never regret.

> Friendship . . . is born at the moment when one man says to another, "What! You too? I thought that no one but myself . . ."
>
> —C. S. Lewis, *The Four Loves*

SCRIPTURE MEMORIZATION FOR WEEK 3

He did not enter by means of the blood of goats and calves; but he entered the Most Holy Place once for all by his own blood, thus obtaining eternal redemption.

—Hebrews 9:12

PRAYER

Dear Father, thank You for Your gift of friendship, and thank You for the friendships I have with other believers. Help me to better appreciate my friends, and strengthen me to be a better friend for others, especially those who are also going through their adoptive journey. In Jesus' name, amen.

DAY 4

Patience

Be completely humble and gentle; be patient, bearing with one another in love.

—Ephesians 4:2

They're not a bad kid behaving badly. They're a traumatized kid, speaking and behaving out of their trauma.

—Mike Berry, "Am I Causing My Child's Behavior to Escalate?" *Confessions of An Adoptive Parent* blog

THE DAILY GIVE AND TAKE

"I've been struck by how similar the relationship is with my sons and me, and my relationship with God, mostly through how I discipline and reward my children," Cecil told me one afternoon.

Cecil and I met years ago through a mutual friend. A few years ago, Cecil, who is single, studied to become a foster parent with the intention of adopting. He specifically asked for those children who after many tries hadn't found the right family yet. Cecil's life changed when his first son arrived. It took a while, but they settled, found their normal, and now his adoption is official. Cecil continues to accept foster care placements and looks forward to adopting again.

"I can go from one to ten in an instant with my children for something as simple as leaving the light on. God gives me so many more chances than I give my sons. I would have given up on me an awful long time ago," Cecil said.

It's all about patience. A component of the fruit of the Spirit (see Galatians 5:22–23), patience pushes us into uncomfortable places as we see how short our fuse can be over the simplest things—especially when we're tired, stressed, or weary. But it's important as we go along on this adoption journey because our children need us to be patient, as God is patient with us.

As we consider how to be patient, Psalm 30:5 gives us a good reminder of what it should look like: "His anger lasts only a moment, but his favor lasts a lifetime; weeping may stay for the night, but rejoicing comes in the morning."

Part of patience includes admitted when we've been impatient, as Cecil recognized in his own parenting. "I have apologized to my sons for losing it with them. And they have apologized to me. We apologize a lot around here," he said.

Children, in general, seem to have a unique talent for prompting an already tired and emotional parent to lose it. Given the traumatic backgrounds most children from foster care or institutional systems come from, the hurt they have endured over time has naturally resulted in their hurting others. They seem to know just the button to push at exactly the worst time. Which parent among us hasn't found themselves in the awkward position of guilt as they reflect on what just transpired, often for things like leaving the light on . . . again? But the greatest reward in our quest for patience with our children is that it only brings us closer to our heavenly Father.

1. Has patience become an issue in your home? How?

2. Do you readily apologize to your children? Why or why not?

3. In what ways have you seen patience help you in your adoptive journey?

4. Read the following Scriptures. How does each describe patience?

Proverbs 14:29

Proverbs 16:32

1 Corinthians 13:4–5

BIBLICAL PATIENCE

Patience has always been a bit of a challenge for me, but it became more so when I became a parent. With concerted effort, determination, and a lot of help from the Holy Spirit, I have become better about it, though I remain a work in progress.

A friend and I were catching up not long ago, and we spent time talking about our family members, taking the time to describe each child. I shared how I was struggling with patience. Since she appeared to serve her family well, I asked what she could share with me about it. She thought a while before she answered.

First, she thanked me for blessing her. She had never really considered herself a patient person, let alone a patient parent. Then she said something that has stayed with me ever since.

"I guess it begins with humility, you know? Why do I get to raise my beautiful boys?" she asked. "I mean, they're really His, yet I get to love them, raise them, and enjoy them. That is usually at the front of my mind. I *get* to serve my family. It keeps me humble. I believe that helps me with patience."

Humility as the key to patience? Her confession was so simple and yet profound. My friend's explanation put me on a quest to discover more about patience. As I studied and prayed, I learned three important lessons about attaining biblical patience, especially as it pertains to parenting.

Patience begins by seeking God.

The disciples witnessed Jesus do the miraculous, yet they asked Him to teach them to pray (not to perform miracles), as recorded in Luke 11:1–4. When I spend time with God, everything about my Christian character here on earth comes into sharper focus. Only with His Spirit can I truly be reminded of who I am—His disciple. He has instructed me in patience, and He will strengthen my desire and ability to grow and practice it better. Whenever I feel myself losing patience or humility, I return to God's presence, where I can be filled once more.

Patience grows as I die to my old self.

Paul reminded us in 2 Corinthians 5:17 that we are no longer who we used to be. The old me was filled with pride and impatience. That part of me died, so I have to make sure it doesn't get resurrected! We can only truly obtain humility when we put to death our egos. Humbleness is at the core of our being able to be patient with our family, with others, with God, and with ourselves.

Patience continues as I defeat pride.

Pride tears away at the fabric of patience. Ecclesiastes 7:8 tells us patience is better than pride. Being patient with our children means we have to go on their schedules, their abilities, and their rate of healing—not on what we determine they should be.

I have found pride has a funny way of rearing its ugly head. However, the one question that helps me keep it buried is this: Am I modeling the kind of behavior I long to see in my children? This question gets at the heart of the issue—the sincerest desire of my heart is how I live in front of my children, my spouse, and others. Defeating my pride keeps me on my knees and actively pursuing my Savior.

I'm thankful God understands our weaknesses. "Let us not become weary in doing good, for at the proper time we will reap a harvest if we do not give up. Therefore, as we have opportunity, let us do good to all people, especially to those who belong to the family of believers" (Galatians 6:9–10). His spirit enables us to be patient parents.

5. When have you struggled as a parent with patience?

6. Are you modeling the kind of behavior you long to see in your children?

7. In what areas do you need to practice modeling better patience to your children?

8. Read each Scripture and answer the corresponding question.

   Proverbs 16:32: What is patience compared to in this verse?

   Romans 12:12: When are we to be patient?

Colossians 3:12: What are we to clothe ourselves with?

STRUGGLING WITH PATIENCE

When I think of my struggle with developing a mature sense of patience, I find my mind wandering to the Book of Job. What a hard but beautiful story. It has to be one of the best stories of patience ever recorded.

Regardless of his loss—his home, his great wealth, and most significantly his children—Job did not blame God but decided to wait on Him to reveal His plan or purpose. That isn't only an amazing amount of faith, that's an incredible amount of trust and patience.

Job was able to be patient because He trusted God to be faithful. Regardless of our family strife and trauma or how many catastrophes we seem to experience in the midst of our adoption journey, we must be patient and trust that God has our best interest at the very heart of His plans for us. This is what enables our patience. This is what matures our faith. This is why our daily relationship with Him is so important.

To love God is to know God. To know him is to be in His Word, to trust that He is faithful, and to be patient that He will show up in our lives, working for our best. Then we too can say with Job, "Blessed be the name of the LORD" (Job 1:21 AMP).

> There's something about patience that God deems necessary for our life in the age to come. And so, whether through agriculture or discipleship or bodily development or eschatology or procreation, God makes us wait.
>
> —Russell D. Moore, *Adopted for Life: The Priority of Adoption for Christian Families and Churches*

9. Where are you in regard to practicing patience?

10. Where would you like to be?

11. What's stopping you from pursuing patience more?

12. In what areas can you ask God for strength to be more patient?

SCRIPTURE MEMORIZATION FOR WEEK 3

He did not enter by means of the blood of goats and calves; but he entered the Most Holy Place once for all by his own blood, thus obtaining eternal redemption.

—Hebrews 9:12

PRAYER

Dear Father, You are the patient parent. You are merciful beyond what I deserve. Please forgive me for my lack of patience. Help me be a better listener to the Spirit's voice in my life when He encourages me to be patient and humble. In Jesus' name, amen.

DAY 5

The Newly Extended Family Journey

Ruth replied, "Don't urge me to leave you or to turn back from you. Where you go I will go, and where you stay I will stay. Your people will be my people and your God my God."

—Ruth 1:16

Whenever we have trouble loving one another, it's usually because we've forgotten how much God loves us.

—Liz Curtis Higgs, *The Girl's Still Got It: Take a Walk with Ruth and the God Who Rocked Her World*

I WILL BE THERE FOR YOU

When we adopt, we often think we're getting specific children, and that's it. But the reality of adoption is that very few of us adopt without introduction to biological family members. Some come into our lives for a short while. Others are with us longer. That was the case with our son's half-sister Svetlana.

I hated leaving Svetlana behind in Ukraine. She was considered an adult, yet my heart ached for her. She never had a mother, had lived on her own for most of her life, and tried hard to be a grown up, even though, in many ways, she was still a child.

My worries over her increased when she'd developed a persistent cough while Jake and I were still in Ukraine. I encouraged her to seek medical attention, but she refused. While my mother-heart wanted to make her take care of herself, I also knew I had to let her be.

The last time I saw her while in Ukraine completing the adoption of Sasha, she was moving into an apartment with a friend. I helped her purchase a few items, such as pots and pans and silverware. As we parted ways, I hugged her tightly. She was carrying a huge bag of kitchen items. I remember how small she looked to me, especially carrying that large bag. I was concerned about her taking the bus and was trying to convince her to allow me to get her a taxi instead. She gave me her *don't-be-ridiculous* look. I knew that look well.

"Please, stay in touch, Svetlana," I said. "Even though I will be living in the US again, that doesn't mean we can't still be a family. I will always be there for you. I will just be your American mama."

"My American mama," she repeated. I couldn't tell if the thought made her happy or simply amused.

"I will miss you," Svetlana said.

I hugged her one last time. She quickly turned away from me and walked toward the bus stop, with the pans clanging as she hurried. Whenever she became emotional, she quickly turned away. I couldn't help but wonder if I would ever see her again.

I was surprised when, two years after I had returned to the States, I received a phone call from her. She'd finally taken my advice to see a doctor, but the visit hadn't gone well. She had been diagnosed with tuberculosis. Now she wanted me to return to Ukraine to be with her for comfort and support—she was reaching out to me as a child reaches out to a mother.

More than her wanting someone beside her for comfort, I knew she also needed someone to help her figure out how best to navigate this scary journey. Even though she asked me to go to her, I wasn't fully convinced I should leave my family, who also needed me and were still healing from trauma.

I went to God with my questions, concerns, and fears. I told Him everything. One thought kept entering my prayers: *I promised I would always be there for her.*

Remembering the promise that day at the bus stop, how could I not go to her? It couldn't be someone else. I knew it had to be me. I started to mentally prepare myself for my return to Ukraine.

Adoption often involves sacrifice. Sometimes those sacrifices extend to the biological family of your adopted children. I couldn't shy away from that. Yet the cost of loving someone is to be willing to be there for them (and their family), encourage them, and simply love them, even at great cost to yourself and to the others you love.

It is part of our Christian mission to love others as Christ loves us (see Matthew 25:31–46). Jesus made it clear in His parable about the sheep and the goats, that how we respond to those in need will be considered in heaven's final judgment. He let us know that while serving those in need, we are actually serving Him.

Even though difficult, it is often a blessing in disguise, just as it was with Svetlana.

1. Were there any biological family members, other than your adopted children, involved in your adoption process? If so, how did it affect your adoption, if at all?

2. If not, do you wish any were involved? Who and for what purpose?

3. Read the following Scripture passages and write how each compels us to care for others.

   Luke 6:31

John 15:13

1 John 4:19

THE JOURNEY TOGETHER

I love the Book of Ruth. When I think of being there for someone, family or not, I think of how Ruth remained steadfast to Naomi.

As a refresher, this Old Testament book starts with a Jewish family who left their homeland of Bethlehem during a famine and moved to Moab, where there was food. They had two sons, who both married Moabite women, one of whom was Ruth. While in Moab, the father and both of the sons died, leaving three widows. Naomi, the matriarch of the family, decided she needed to return to Bethlehem, and Ruth determined to go with her.

News of Naomi's return and her daughter-in-law Ruth's loyalty must have spread around Bethlehem, because one of their kinship-redeemers, Boaz, remarked in Ruth 2:11 that he had heard of Ruth's kind treatment of Naomi. Then Boaz spoke a blessing over her for it.

As the story progressed, Ruth and Boaz began a courtship and were married. And we see that Ruth, a foreigner and Gentile (a Moabite) became the great-grandmother of King David and is in the lineage of Jesus. Ruth's loyalty to Naomi was rewarded both with a new husband, a new life in Bethlehem, and a place in history as part of the family of the Messiah Himself.

Through her steadfastness and concern for Naomi, Ruth displayed her character. The Book of Ruth is a beautiful illustration of God bringing Gentiles into His family with Himself and the Jewish people. God also shows how much He loves both men and women, showing no indifference to Ruth and Naomi's plight. But what I love most about the Book of Ruth is how it illustrates the role of a Redeemer in our lives. It's a beautiful picture: Boaz redeeming Ruth, preserving the lineage both Boaz and her late husband shared, and Jesus redeeming the church, His bride, through His sacrifice for us.

We are often asked to sacrifice before, during, and after our adoption journey. We have been redeemed, and we help others reconcile and find that redemption.

As Paul wrote in Ephesians 5:2: "Walk in the way of love, just as Christ loved us and gave himself up for us as a fragrant offering and sacrifice to God." As He sacrificed for us, we must in turn, sacrifice for others, including our newly extended family, so that we honor both our adopted children and our heavenly Father.

4. Read the Book of Ruth. What part of Ruth's story speaks most to you, regarding your adoption journey?

5. How does your family sacrifice for each other?

6. How does each of the following Scripture passages describe sacrifice for others?

   Romans 12:1

   Philippians 2:5–8

Hebrews 13:16

SACRIFICIAL TOGETHERNESS

Becoming a family takes time and a great deal of empathy for one another. Creating a family bond demands constant attention through sacrifice, focused activities, and even family counseling. It reminds me of 1 Corinthians 12:26 (ESV), where Paul stated, "If one member suffers, all suffer together; if one member is honored, all rejoice together."

Sometimes bonding as a new family takes place during times of sacrifice. I know that our family's decision to sacrifice to help Svetlana helped us bond together. We prayed together about her for many nights. We looked forward to updates on how she was doing. Our whole family sacrificed when I traveled to see her. Families sacrifice for one another.

In our days and times of sacrifice, may we always be reminded of the great sacrifice God made for us to join His family. I need to be reminded. I want to be reminded. Such an incredible gift and such great cost. Thank You, Father.

> Like our Savior, who poured out His life and blood so we have reason to rejoice, we were made to lay down our lives and give until it hurts.
>
> —Francis Chan, *Forgotten God: Reversing Our Tragic Neglect of the Holy Spirit*

7. How does your family bond together?

8. What seems to help your family relationships?

9. In what ways can you more actively bond?

SCRIPTURE MEMORIZATION FOR WEEK 3

He did not enter by means of the blood of goats and calves; but he entered the Most Holy Place once for all by his own blood, thus obtaining eternal redemption.

—Hebrews 9:12

PRAYER

Dear Father, thank You for redeeming me. Thank You for allowing me the privilege of imitating You, in a small way, through adoption. Give me strength and wisdom when our days are rough. May Your mercy and forgiveness be evident in me, especially to those You have given me to love. In Jesus' name, amen.

WEEK 4

The Legality Realized

DAY 1
What's in a Name?

For you [who are born-again have been reborn from above—spiritually transformed, renewed, sanctified and] are all children of God [set apart for His purpose with full rights and privileges] through faith in Christ Jesus.

—Galatians 3:26 AMP

But, if I may reference Inigo Montoya from *The Princess Bride*, I do not think *orphan* means what we think it means. . . . The word is so much broader and more expansive than we give it credit for.

—Lorilee Craker, *Anne of Green Gables, My Daughter and Me: What My Favorite Book Taught Me about Grace, Belonging and the Orphan in Us All*

THE LEGALITY OF IT ALL

I will always remember the day our son's adoption was legalized. We had to wade through many portions of the process—both here in the United States and overseas in his birth country. First, we had to legally adopt him in Ukraine, which took two years in the making. Then we had to officially change his name so we could obtain his new Ukrainian passport and then hand it to the US consulate in order to obtain his visa to the States—that took one year in the making. The last step was for him to hand over a sealed package from the US consulate, in Kiev, Ukraine, to the US Customs and Border Protection office in the Chicago O'Hare airport—less than two weeks in the making. Finally, our son's certificate of naturalization came in the mail weeks later. With that certificate, we could then order his

Michigan birth certificate and Social Security card. *Finally*, he was legally our son and a citizen of the United States. Lots of legal procedures just to be able to call him our son!

I had anticipated his adoption to be a more straightforward process and to happen in a shorter timeframe. I expected it to be easier. Looking back, however, I'm amazed we were able to manage it at all!

Our son's adoption was nothing less than a miracle. An orphan from birth, coupled with living in an Eastern European orphanage for nearly the first four years of his life, was no small feat to survive. Out of the entire orphanage staff, only one caretaker seemed to have a heart for our small son. Seeing the state of the children in the orphanage and the lack of staff compassion, I'm amazed he smiled at all. It is still difficult for me to comprehend what the children experience. It made me ache for all the children, but especially for our son, whom I wished we could have adopted sooner.

And the only thing keeping him there versus placing him in my arms? The legality of his adoption. That change of his name. Signatures released him and signatures claimed him so he would be an orphan no longer.

It seems so simple, and yet the process does not come without a great price. The same can be said for our spiritual adoption. That too has legalities that must be attended too. A price paid, a signature in blood to claim us, and we are orphans no longer.

I rejoiced when the little orphan boy became our forever son. I rejoiced again when he sought a second adoption—that of joining God's spiritual family. He asked for God's forgiveness for his sinful ways, and he accepted Christ as his Savior. Our son is now a son of God. Sin no longer separates him from his Maker. His name has been entered into the Book of Life. Our son is His, and we are but caregivers.

Without the legal act of adoption, I cannot imagine what my son's life would be like. His adoption makes him a son, a brother, a grandson, a nephew, and a cousin. The network of people who love him could hardly be found in any other way. God knows this, and that is why He adopted us. To be brought into family is the most intimate way to love. That is why adoption remains the best form of orphan care.

    1. According to Galatians 3:26, who are called the children of God?

2. How did your spiritual adoption change your life?

3. How do the following Scriptures describe your legality as a child of God?

Deuteronomy 27:9

Proverbs 14:26

Matthew 5:9

When the fullness of time had come, God sent forth his Son, born of woman, born under the law, to redeem those who were under the law, so that we might receive adoption as sons.

—Galatians 4:4–5 ESV

OUR SPIRITUAL LEGAL STATUS

In Galatians 4:5, *adoption*, translated from the Greek word *huiothesia*, literally means "to place as a son." According to *Vines Lexicon*, the word means "the place and condition of a son given to one to whom it does not naturally belong." In addition, The *Holman Christian Standard Bible* translates it to mean "the legal act whereby a child is accepted into a family on an equal basis—including the same rights of inheritance—with any physical offspring of the parents."

During that period in which Paul wrote, adoption meant the adopted person was permanently placed in the family. When God wrote through Paul that we were *huiothesia*, he was reassuring us that we were chosen, that our place in God's family is permanent, and that the process was a legal one. In fact, the adopted relationship was considered even more permanent than that of birth.

William M. Ramsey, a Roman culture historian, explained it this way in his book *A Historical Commentary on St. Paul's Epistle to the Galatians*:

> The Roman-Syrian Law-Book . . . where a formerly prevalent Greek law had persisted under the Roman Empire—well illustrates this passage of the Epistle. It actually lays down the principle that a man can never put away an adopted son, and that he cannot put away a real son without good ground. It is remarkable that the adopted son should have a stronger position than the son by birth, yet it was so.

I find it amazing to think of our spiritual adoption that way. God's promise to us is so binding it cannot be undone. You and I are legally His. We are permanently His.

4. Reflect on our position in God's family. How does it make you feel to consider that God has chosen you and you belong to Him permanently?

5. Does today's study change the way you previously viewed your spiritual adoption? In what ways?

6. According to Galatians 3:26, what is the only way we can enter God's family?

7. Read the following Scripture passages, then answer each question.

   Luke 6:35: How are we to show we are sons of the Most High?

   John 1:12–13: Who did God give the right to become children of God?

   Romans 8:14: Who are the sons of God?

8. In light of this understanding of our spiritual adoption, in what ways does it change how you act?

I AM ADOPTED

When I think of all the times Satan has lied to me, I'm surprised. Not by the fact that Satan has lied; after all, the Bible tells us he is "a liar and the father of lies" (John 8:44), so that's what he does. I'm surprised by my gullibility to his lies, especially those that fall under the "you're not really a Christian" category.

Every time I hear a speaker at a conference or read a book about my spiritual adoption, I am confronted with the truth: I am a daughter of the Most High. His spiritual adoption of me has made this an undeniable claim (Galatians 4:4–7). No whispers from Satan can erase God's declaration of love for me. Or for you.

What more can be said of adoption than it is love made visible, legal, and permanent? What more can be written than our names in the Book of Life? What more is needed than the strength of our Father's arms?

You and I are adopted. We are His through our faith in Jesus Christ. Our eternity is legally sealed by and because of His blood shed for us—the payment to make it legally binding. The legality of our adoption into His family—that is what makes all the difference.

> Without the actual act of legal adoption, a child will forever live with the very real pain and fear of being alone. The need for permanence is a huge, gaping need—the cry of countless hearts across the globe. It is a cry that throbs, that aches, that longs . . . and it is a cry the Father is calling us to answer.
>
> —(late) Derek Loux, adoptive father and blogger, "The Cry the Father Is Calling Us to Answer," *Jon and Kinsey* blog

SCRIPTURE MEMORIZATION FOR WEEK 4

And, "I will be a Father to you, and you will be my sons and daughters, says the Lord Almighty."

—2 Corinthians 6:18

PRAYER

Dear Father, through Your mercy to me, I praise You for paying my sin debt, for redeeming me, and legally adopting me as Your own child. Just as I have adopted my child legally and consider that a permanent condition, thank You for Your love for me that will not let me go. In Jesus' name, amen.

DAY 2

Loved . . . No Matter What

The LORD your God is with you, the Mighty Warrior who saves. He will take great delight in you; in his love he will no longer rebuke you, but will rejoice over you with singing.

—Zephaniah 3:17

Because of grace we have nothing to prove. Our confidence is in the security and power God gives us, not in ourselves. To know that you are absolutely treasured, unconditionally, changes you in this way.

—Jennie Allen, *Restless: Because You Were Made for More*

WHY DON'T I DESERVE A FAMILY?

A number of adoptions happen through our foster care system, and when it works well, hundreds of children are able to find forever families. Unfortunately, too often reports indicate these systems are grossly below funding standards, and the staff struggles to meet the legal needs of all concerned.

One child, Mandy, knew the downside of the over-burdened system only too well. Abandoned and abused, Mandy just couldn't understand why she wasn't able to be placed with a family who wanted her. She saw other children from foster care find forever families, but it seemed as though she just kept getting passed over.

She finally was adopted when she was nine, but for years, she suffered through the heartache of feeling nobody wanted her.

Now, an adult, Mandy is a mother of seventeen children—fifteen of whom she has adopted—an inspirational speaker, an adoption advocate, and my prayer partner.

As we were talking one day about adoption and the complex US foster care system, she shared with me those feelings of not being wanted. "What did I do to not deserve a family?" Mandy asked. "That's how I felt. I just couldn't understand it."

Mandy felt guilty about not being adopted, as though she were the problem. People kept telling her it wasn't her fault, but in her young mind, it *was* all about her. Everything that was happening was happening to her, so it was personal.

When she was finally adopted, she still struggled with the feelings of belonging and of being wanted, of really feeling as though she were part of a family. When her parents took her to church, she was surprised by the message she heard the pastor preach.

He was speaking on Zephaniah 3:17, which says He "will rejoice over you with singing." Those words caught her attention. "Think about that," she said. "He *rejoices* over me. It was as if the scales of hopelessness and never measuring up fell away, and God's Word came alive. I felt like that pastor was talking directly to me." Her pastor explained that God had loved her before anything had happened in her life, before any of the brokenness, and before she was even born. He talked about how nothing could ever separate her from God and His love.

Mandy asked her new mom if God really meant it. Her mother assured her that yes, God did mean it, and then taught her Romans 8:37–39: "In all these things we are more than conquerors through him who loved us. For I am convinced that neither death nor life, neither angels nor demons, neither the present nor the future, nor any powers, neither height nor depth, nor anything else in all creation, will be able to separate us from the love of God that is in Christ Jesus our Lord."

Suddenly, Mandy's world blew open. She belonged! She knew God had created her for a purpose, and nothing could separate her from Him.

For the traumatized child, it is all about trust and trusting God's love. This understanding brought a whole new life to Mandy, something she now works to help children, especially those in the foster care system, to see—God is trustworthy. This is especially true for a child who feels a great many things but doesn't feel loved.

1. How is God described in Zephaniah 3:17?

2. What part of Mandy's story have you experienced or witnessed?

3. Read each Scripture, and describe God's steadfast love for us.

   Deuteronomy 4:31

   Psalm 94:14

   Hebrews 13:5

THE LOVINGKINDNESS OF GOD

Throughout Psalms, King David wrote and sang of God's lovingkindness, His steadfast love.

> We have thought of thy lovingkindness, O God, in the midst of thy temple.
>
> —Psalm 48:9 KJV

The Hebrew word *checed* was used in the Bible to explain how God cared for His loved ones. This word is often translated into "lovingkindness," as it is in Psalm 48:9, meaning redemption from enemies and also redemption from sin.

We need to understand steadfast and everlasting are not only a part of His nature but a descriptor of Him as a being. Just as with adopted children, security is an important part of our need. His lovingkindness, His steadfast, everlasting love for us, perfectly fills the void we experience apart from Him.

God's lovingkindness contains the element of divine mercy (Titus 3:4–6). We do not get what we deserve—punishment for our failings. Instead, in God we find incredible pardon and a love beyond measure.

God's lovingkindness contains a covenant of loyalty to us. We can take great comfort in knowing God has pledged His love to us, and that pledge will not end.

God's lovingkindness contains benevolence. It includes God's whole-hearted devotion to His people. God will love us "exceeding abundantly above all that we ask or think" (Ephesians 3:20 KJV).

Our eternal God offers this incredible lovingkindness to His children. Why? Because we belong to Him. This is what our adoptive Father offers us. This covenant of eternal love is our legitimacy, our legality, as His sons and daughters. We are loved.

4. How would you describe God's lovingkindness to you?

5. Read each Scripture and consider how God and His lovingkindness is described.

Nehemiah 9:17

Psalm 36:7

Isaiah 54:8

OUR NEED

We have an innate need for security. In his 1943 paper, "A Theory of Human Motivation," Abraham Maslow described it as a hierarchy of needs, set in a particular order, security being among the most basic. Jesus described our need for God as a thirst in John 4:13–14, "Everyone who drinks this water will be thirsty again, but whoever drinks the water I give them will never thirst. Indeed, the water I give them will become in them a spring of water welling up to eternal life." Where we find security is where we can thrive.

It is the same for our children. They find their security in the adults in their life. As my friend, Mandy, said, however, even though we can offer security and our physical presence, we can let them down.

How wonderful it is that we can lead them to our Savior—the one who can fulfill every longing, the one who will never let them down. He has chosen us as parents to share His lovingkindness and the sense of belonging to our children. Through us, they can glimpse their heavenly Father who loves them *no matter what*.

> There are no "if's" in God's world. And no places that are safer than other places. The center of His will is our only safety . . . let us pray that we may always know it!
>
> —Corrie Ten Boom, *The Hiding Place*

6. Grab a concordance and look up verses that talk about God's love and lovingkindness. Which verse resonates most with you? Why?

7. Why is it so important for children to feel secure? In what ways can you show God's love to them to help them feel that security?

8. If you asked your family, how would they respond that they glimpse God in your daily life? How would you like them to?

SCRIPTURE MEMORIZATION FOR WEEK 4

And, "I will be a Father to you, and you will be my sons and daughters, says the Lord Almighty."

—2 Corinthians 6:18

PRAYER

Dear Father, I want Your love; I crave it in my frailness. I accept Your Word as truth and claim Your promise that nothing can ever separate me from You and Your great love. Help me to introduce and consistently confirm Your great love to my children. May we never lose sight of You and Your great love for us, no matter what. In Jesus' name, amen.

DAY 3

Explaining the Process

I will be a Father to you, and you will be my sons and daughters, says the Lord Almighty.

—2 Corinthians 6:18

How awesome of God to purpose that Christ's royal lineage would come through His adoptive father. We shouldn't be surprised at the profound significance with which God views adoption. Ephesians 1:4–6 tells us something profound about God's view of adoption. It identifies us as the adopted children of God. In a peculiar kind of way, God the Father allowed His Son to be "adopted" into a family on earth so that we could be adopted into His family in heaven.

—Beth Moore, *Jesus, the One and Only*

ADOPTED AND ADOPTED AGAIN

Adoptive families often find themselves explaining the different elements of adoption. Those explanations offer a loving perspective to an otherwise legal process. It gives families a chance to break down the elements that directly affect the children involved. My friends, Christy and David, faced such a situation.

My family and I attend the same church as Christy and David, so I was able to witness their foster-care work firsthand. They have fostered six children so far, but Bella was their first adoption.

Christy said the first thing she and David wanted six-year-old Bella to know was what was happening to her, this change from being their foster child to becoming their adopted daughter. They started with her name change.

Bella loves Bible stories, so they used the name changes God gave Abram (to Abraham) and Sarai (to Sarah), in Genesis 17:5–15. They explained, just as God changed their names, they were changing hers. Bella loves her new name and its meaning—*beautiful.*

Next, Christy and David tackled the concept of a forever family. They did their best to put it into terms she could understand. They explained that nothing she could do or say would change their love for her, just as nothing we can do or say can remove us from God's family. Forever is a commitment, they told her. They don't stop being a family or loving one another just because one of them is having a bad day.

"We wanted to meet Bella exactly where she is," Christy said. "Just as God meets us."

Bella absorbed everything. She had been part of their lives for nearly three years by the time her adoption was completed. She had looked forward to it but also seemed to recognize the serious nature of it.

Christy noticed Bella leaning toward God before the adoption. When her birth mother made poor choices, those choices resulted in Bella not being able to see her anymore. In response, Bella told Christy, "She needs Jesus."

Christy asked her if she knew what that meant and then explained how they had been adopted into God's family. They admitted to God they were sinners and accepted Jesus as their Savior. "When you're ready to do that," Christy told Bella, "you let me know."

"I'm ready now," Bella said.

"I wonder if Bella's earthly adoption makes her spiritual adoption even more special for her," Christy told me. "I don't think I will ever appreciate my spiritual adoption the way she does. Somehow, it makes it more . . . real."

She made a good point. I wondered if I too take my spiritual adoption for granted.

I know my spiritual adoption has been made more real to me since we adopted our son. I believe God likes to surprise us in this way. We think we are only helping someone else, when in truth, we ourselves are being helped.

1. In Galatians 4:6, it is written, "Because you are his sons, God sent the Spirit of his Son into our hearts, the Spirit who calls out, 'Abba, Father.'" According to this Scripture, why have we been sent His spirit?

2. Reread Beth Moore's quote from the beginning of this chapter. Now in your own words, rephrase what she is saying about adoption.

3. Read each Scripture below, and describe what Christ has done for us.

   Romans 8:30

   Ephesians 5:27

   Colossians 1:22

4. Read Ephesians 1:3–14, paying attention to verses 5–6. What do these verses mean to you?

TO THE PRAISE OF HIS GLORIOUS GRACE

Before God created us, He planned for our redemption. To those who would chose to love and follow Him, God predestined them with the grace to become His children by adoption through their faith in Jesus.

Our adoption was always God's plan for us. Before the creation of the world and the creation of humans, He expressed His love for us by planning our adoption. There is nothing we did to deserve it.

Our adoption comes through Jesus Christ. That means in order for us to be adopted by God, we have to accept Christ's death as our redemptive payment.

> God presented Christ as a sacrifice of atonement, through the shedding of his blood—to be received by faith. He did this to demonstrate his righteousness, because in his forbearance he had left the sins committed beforehand unpunished—he did it to demonstrate his righteousness at the present time, so as to be just and the one who justifies those who have faith in Jesus.
>
> —Romans 3:25–26

The goal of our adoption was "to the praise of his glorious grace" (Ephesians 1:6). Nothing else can satisfy our souls apart from glorifying God. "Now if we are children, then we are heirs—heirs of God and co-heirs with Christ, if indeed we share in his sufferings in order that we may also share in his glory" (Romans 8:17).

The entire first chapter of Ephesians comes to life when we realize this simple yet powerful truth: Our adoption is from Him, through Him, and to Him. Our spiritual adoption is glorious and lasting, thanks to Jesus Christ.

5. When did God plan to adopt us?

6. What did He redeem us from?

7. Read each Scripture below and answer the corresponding question.

   Matthew 25:34: At what time will those on His right inherit the kingdom prepared for them?

   Colossians 1:22: In what way did Christ die to present us?

   2 Timothy 1:9: How are we called?

WHEN THE LEGAL CHANGE IS LIFE SAVING

There are times when adoptions don't go as planned. Sometimes due to changing paperwork. Sometimes due to mistakes. Sometimes due to changes in the law.

This was true for hundreds of US families in 2012 when Americans were prohibited from adopting Russian children. My friend, Samantha, and her family were one of the families affected. They had already flown to Russia and met their soon-to-be-adopted daughter, Victoria, and loved her, in spite of her medical condition, known as hemiplegia. Their adoption was interrupted just before it was completed, and Victoria was moved to a foster home in Russia, where she later died.

After months of healing, Samantha and her family changed to Ukraine. They were surprised when they were taken to visit a girl in a mental institution, instead of an orphanage. They noticed young girls standing by the entrance. One of the girls, Allison, stood out from the others. She had a bright light in her eyes. When they learned she had the same hemiplegia condition Victoria had, they could hardly believe it.

Allison is now their daughter. She has received two life-saving heart surgeries. It has affected Samantha's walk with God. She has started a hosting program for children waiting for adoption from Ukraine to the United States.

"I have become closer to God during our journey of adoption. Helping children lost in the system has become my calling. I have begun to recognize the spiritual warfare surrounding it," Samantha said.

There is much to be said for the legal process in adoption, in many ways. Regardless, God continues to care for the orphaned, as he did for Allison. She is evidence God can turn anything for good, as it is written in Genesis 50:20, "You intended to harm me, but God intended it for good to accomplish what is now being done, the saving of many lives."

> I pray, "Lord do I have a faith reckless enough to believe you have always had a plan for [the orphans]?" I feel him answering back, "Do you have a faith strong enough to want to be a part of my plan?"
>
> —Beth Guckenberger, *Restless Faith: Let Go and Be Led*

8. Do you have a scheduled time to meet with God? If not, can you begin to include God in your daily schedule?

9. Reflect on how God planned for us to be reconciled through adoption into His family. Write how understanding that reconciliation and adoption changes the way you think about your role in His family and how you can plan to include God in your daily schedule.

SCRIPTURE MEMORIZATION FOR WEEK 4

And, "I will be a Father to you, and you will be my sons and daughters, says the Lord Almighty."

—2 Corinthians 6:18

PRAYER

Dear Father, You are such a loving Father. You chose to adopt me while I was living in sin as Your enemy. There was nothing I could do to reach You. Out of Your love, You reached out to me and held me close. I want to stay close to You, Father. Draw me to You. In Jesus' name, amen.

DAY 4
Unquestionable Redemption

In him we have redemption through his blood, the forgiveness of sins, in accordance with the riches of God's grace.

—Ephesians 1:7

The heavenly Father was not willing to lose His beloved creation to the powers of hell, so He formed a redemption plan—one that came completely from His heart of love, before the world was created.

—David Wilkerson, *It Is Finished: Finding Lasting Victory Over Sin*

EVERYONE IS REDEEMABLE

Before I became a Christian, I remember thinking that others may not want to be my friend if they knew how evil I was in my mind and heart. Without condemnation from anyone else, my elementary school self already recognized how wicked the human heart could be. It took an invitation from a soft-spoken pastor to convince me that Jesus loved me, right where I was, and that I could be forgiven.

Everyone can be forgiven. Most families can find a second chance. The same is true for our country's foster care system. Because it is filled with flawed individuals, it too is flawed. But because God can redeem all people—and institutions—the foster care system has hope.

Tara sat across from me in a coffee shop and she described her first encounter with foster care when she was still in middle school. Her best friend was living in a foster home.

"From my middle-school-aged view, I would say my friend was from a family of origin I would rate as an F. She was being fostered in a B home," said Tara. "When a judge finally allowed her to return to her mom's, her home life had been raised to about a D. And my friend was thrilled. She couldn't wait to go home."

That's when Tara learned that foster care was all about reconciliation. "It didn't matter to my friend what level of home she was in. She was going home. I told my friend back then, 'Someday I'm going to take care of kids like you.'"

Tara's friend knew that everyone was redeemable, including her mom. She recognized her mom needed to change things, and she did, to the best of her ability. And her friend wanted to return to her mom.

Years later, Tara married Jamie and they had their daughter, Anna. When Anna was seven years old, they became foster parents through the local Department of Human Services (DHS). They didn't get called right away, but when they did, it was unforgettable.

Their first placement was Ezra. He came to them from a local hospital's neonatal unit. He was a micro-preemie born addicted to drugs. Of course, foster care is always set up with the hope that the biological family will be able to bring the child back into a safe and loving environment. That was Tara and Jamie's hope as well. But when Ezra's mom stopped visiting him, Tara realized that reconciliation for Ezra was becoming less of an option.

Tara started thinking about adoption. Fortunately, Jamie was on the same page. "This from the man who thought he could never adopt," Tara said. "He took one look at that tiny little guy and knew he would become part of our family. That could only be from God."

They adopted Ezra at the age of sixteen months. To date, they have fostered nine children from DHS and have been pleased when those children have been able to reconcile with their biological families. But they continued to remain open to the possibility that God may call them to adopt another child from foster care, and three years after Ezra's adoption, Isaac joined their family.

"I am no different from any of the birth parents I have encountered," said Tara. "I have simply been reconciled to God, redeemed. Foster care will show you that you need redemption, let me tell you. It can bring out the worst in you. Your need for redemption, your need for Jesus, *will* show up."

That gift of redemption always played in Tara's mind while she was fostering. Her family always prayed for the birth parents. She desperately wanted her sons to witness redemption in the lives of the children who returned to their families. She got her chance when she started foster care for yet another baby boy.

DHS called Tara and asked if she would relieve another foster mother. The youngest of four brothers would not stop crying. It was making care for the older three boys difficult. Tara agreed to take the baby. Tara saw the four boys all together when she picked him up. She decided then and there she wanted to meet with their birth mother, Veronica.

The two mothers met and Tara shared that she wanted to help reunify Veronica's family. She encouraged Veronica, even though she knew it was going to require a great deal of commitment. Veronica agreed to try.

With hard work of her own, and help and encouragement from Tara and others, Veronica did have all four of her boys returned to her. She said God sent her a team of people to let her know it was possible. Tara was part of that team.

"I loved on Veronica, and God did the rest. He redeemed her. Isn't that what we're supposed to be about?"

We all have a redemption story, a second chance. Our spiritual redemption story becomes even more real when we get to witness or hear of a physical, human redemption story.

1. In what ways would our churches be impacted if they were truly willing to be the first place to help children in crisis?

2. What part of Tara's story do you identify with? Why?

3. Read the following Scriptures and write how each describes our redemption.

   1 Corinthians 1:30

Galatians 3:13

1 Peter 1:18–19

4. Read Hebrews 10:11–18. How should we describe the legality of our adoption by God?

ONCE AND FOR ALL

Think about the absoluteness of our redemption. The legality of it. The eternal in it—especially in Hebrews 10:14: "For by one sacrifice he has made perfect *forever* those who are being made holy" (emphasis added).

The Miniature Commentary says it this way: "Under the new [covenant], one Sacrifice is enough to procure for all nations and ages, spiritual pardon, or being freed from punishment in the world to come." Freedom from the punishment we deserved in the sinful state we were born. This is the new covenant promised under the Messiah.

But how can this one act of sacrifice last forever? *Barnes' Notes on the Bible* offers this answer: "The offering is of such a character that it secures their final freedom from sin, and will make them forever holy."

Who does it make holy? God's people. In his sermon, "Perfected for All Time by a Single Offering," John Piper explains: "This verse means that you can have assurance that you stand perfected and completed in the eyes of your heavenly Father not because you are perfect now, but precisely because you are not perfect now but are 'being sanctified,' 'being made holy,' that, by faith in God's promises, you are moving away from your lingering imperfection toward more and more holiness."

The sacrifices of the priests in the Old Testament did not last. Adherence to the law did not last. Only the sacrifice of Christ through His blood can cover the sins of the world and endure forever. This is the forever legality of our redemption. This is how our adoption is made possible.

5. Read Jeremiah 31:33–34. In your own words, write what that verse means and how it applies to your redemption.

FOREVER

As a parent, I am used to daily sacrifice. I understand that my children will take for granted and ignore my sacrifices but will still expect me to offer them. I would not exactly describe self-denial as something I love to do, but I don't exactly hate it either. I bear it because I know, in the long run, it promotes an idea of care, nurture, and love to those I love. However, I also understand that parenting is for a season and there is an end in sight.

The concept of forever is a hard one to grasp fully. I can know the concept of forever, of eternity, but I can't really put my mind all the way around it. My thoughts are far too finite to properly understand infinite.

Yet even though I can't fully comprehend forever, it gives me comfort to think that I will spend forever with God. It gives me confidence to consider that His "parenting" of me doesn't have an end in sight, that it isn't just for a season. I find assurance that when my bad days in parenting seem to last forever, and some of them do, they fade in comparison to the foreverness of my God. His forever kind of love gives me strength. When I fall short in my faith, the knowledge of forever restores my hope. The legally sealed, forever aspect of God is yet another reason we can praise and trust Him.

Jesus was born under the law of God and took on himself the condemnation we deserved for our sin. Now the full legal rights of adoption are given to us who are in Christ by faith.

—C. John Miller, *Saving Grace: Daily Devotions from Jack Miller*

6. What is it about the forever concept of God's redemption that brings you the most comfort?

7. Reflect on the concept of our redemption being forever. Write about what first comes to mind.

SCRIPTURE MEMORIZATION FOR WEEK 4

And, "I will be a Father to you, and you will be my sons and daughters, says the Lord Almighty."

—2 Corinthians 6:18

PRAYER

Dear Father, You are my forever God. The sacrifice of Your only Son has made my forever with You possible. Draw me close. Help me to draw my children close to You. May my imperfection only draw them closer to You. Thank You for Your forever love. In Jesus' name, amen.

DAY 5
Creating Family

If anyone has material possessions and sees a brother or sister in need but has no pity on them, how can the love of God be in that person?

—1 John 3:17

God doesn't call us to be comfortable. He calls us to trust Him so completely that we are unafraid to put ourselves in situations where we will be in trouble if He doesn't come through.

—Francis Chan, *Crazy Love: Overwhelmed by a Relentless God*

BECOMING FAMILY

At times, especially during adoption, we can be asked to do things we never thought possible. We experience more. We endure more. We exhaust more.

I experienced that when I said yes when my son's biological sister Svetlana asked me to return to Ukraine and be with her during her tuberculosis testing. Some of the longest minutes of my life were experienced while standing in line at the Odessa airport to reenter Ukraine for the first time since our adoption finalized (it had not gone smoothly).

God, I prayed, *have I made the right decision?*

I was able to reenter Ukraine without incident, and I hurried to meet Svetlana downtown. I wanted her to eat something before she went for testing at the tuberculosis hospital in Odessa.

It was hard for us to communicate. I had lost most of the Russian I'd learned during my previous time in Ukraine. As we sipped our hot tea, I noticed she kept wiping tears away. That's when I realized just how much my being there for her meant.

She insisted on wearing a face mask while with me. For my protection, she said. I could see her face while we ate, however. She had lost weight, and she couldn't afford to. Her petite frame was already beginning to look frail.

When we arrived at the hospital, she filled out the forms at the registration desk. Every once and while, she would look up and smile at me. I wrote my email address in a portion I assumed was for next of kin.

After her testing was complete, I took her grocery shopping and helped her get a taxi home. We made plans to meet again. I was hoping to get her test results before I left.

Looking back now, I believe the most important aspect of my return to Ukraine was that I was able to physically be there for her. The fact that someone was there with her, out of love for her, was the one thing Svetlana needed from me. Though others thought me crazy to return, I knew it was the right thing to do. Yes, she needed to be thoroughly tested and, if needed, receive treatment. But having family—someone caring for her—that was what her heart needed most.

What can speak louder of God's love to a child without family than someone stepping forward in love and becoming family for them?

It became my mission to try and create family for Svetlana, regardless of what her test results revealed. God had placed her in my life for a reason. I wanted to be obedient and care for her the way I would want to be cared for. Even from a long distance, I asked God to help me care for her as a daughter. If not officially adopted, then as a vulnerable child needing care.

God answered my prayers, though not as I had hoped.

1. Reread today's opening Scripture. How does 1 John 3:17 mandate Christians to act?

2. Read each Scripture, and explain how it encourages us.

Proverbs 22:9

Luke 6:38

Galatians 6:2

A NEW COMMAND TO CARE

After our redemption was paid, God legally adopted us into His family. With our adoption comes all our legal rights. But it also comes with guidelines for us to live by. A mandate to die to ourselves. A mandate to care for orphans. A mandate to love one another. All of these guidelines are placed there for our good—and God asks that we perform them not out of mere duty, but because we love our heavenly Father.

The Bible teaches us that we ought to love our neighbor as ourselves (see Leviticus 19:18). That is a high command. We love ourselves most, yet Christ commanded something more.

In John 13, when Jesus was speaking to His disciples, He was preparing to leave them. He knew His time on earth was coming to an end, so He left them with a new commandment, one that commanded even more than loving our neighbors as ourselves.

In John 13:34 (*The Message*), Jesus said, "Let me give you a new command: Love one another. In the same way I loved you, you love one another." This new command raised the love aspect to a whole new level. Jesus was no longer suggesting that we love others as we love ourselves; He was commanding us to love others as *Jesus* loved. That would take beyond a lifetime. How could one ever hope to check that off a list here on earth?

It also changes our motive for caring. Our motive to love now becomes our desire to be more like Him. As His disciples, His love becomes the example we are to follow.

However, Jesus knew we would be unable to follow this new command within our own strength. He made a provision for us so that we *would* be able to love others the way He commanded. When He gave the command, Jesus knew the helper, the Holy Spirit, was coming soon and that He would help us to live out this new commandment. We don't have to wait until we get to heaven to strive toward this goal of loving others.

Our imitation of Christ and His love is our response to becoming His adopted children. Most children attempt to imitate their parents. And with the Spirit's assistance, we find the strength and motivation to love beyond what we in and of ourselves are capable of doing.

But Jesus also provided another reason for us to love that way. In John 13:35, He said, "This is how everyone will recognize that you are my disciples—when they see the love you have for each other." To love like Christ is to show Him to the world. They will see Jesus by how we love. Such a humbling responsibility.

One of my favorite campfire songs is based on John 13:35: "We Are One in the Spirit/They'll Know We Are Christians." It was written in the 1960s by Peter R. Scholtes while he was serving as a priest in Chicago. I have sung that song for decades, but do I live it out? Do I love others the way Jesus loves me? Do I love my children the way Jesus loves me?

We have been commanded to care for those around us—everyone around us and those God places in our path. For me, it is a process. What at first seemed impossible—especially loving those who oversaw nearly every aspect of our adoption journey—has become possible. With the Holy Spirit's continued help, I can love as He loved, every day, and hopefully, someday, without having to think about it.

3. What does loving like Jesus loves mean to you?

4. How does adoption show love as Christ loved?

5. In what areas do you need the Holy Spirit's help to love others as Jesus loves?

6. Read each Scripture, and answer the corresponding question.

1 Peter 1:22: How does Peter suggest we love?

1 John 2:10: How are those who love described?

John 15:12–13: Loving like Christ means what?

LOVE MORE LIKE JESUS

When I think of loving someone as Jesus loves, I think of my family members first. They know how to frustrate me the most, can find my last-nerve buttons, and push them all at once. Lately, I've been focusing on how to respond with more love.

The most important thing about Jesus and His love begins with His humility. If I am not humble in my thoughts and my heart, my actions cannot follow. My total dying to self must kill my prideful ways.

The Apostle Paul offered a strong description of what being humble looks like: "Be completely humble and *gentle*; be *patient*, *bearing with one another* in love" (Ephesians 4:2, emphasis added). When I read that verse, being gentle, patient, and bearing with each other appear as great indicators of humility.

This is how I desire to portray Christ to the world, to my friends, to my family. This is how I can *best* portray Christ to the world. When I went to Ukraine and offered strength and assistance and comfort to Svetlana, I like to think that perhaps I was loving her as Jesus loves and that I portrayed Christ in a beautiful way to her. This is how I live out my undeserved adoption into His family.

> Everything changed in my life when I stopped focusing on my own dreams and purposes, and instead concentrated on walking out God's dreams and purposes for my life.
>
> —Tricia Goyer, *Walk It Out: The Radical Result of Living God's Word One Step at a Time*

7. What part of Ephesians 4:2 speaks loudest to you of humility?

8. In what ways do you need to love more from a place of humility?

9. Reflect on Christ's love for you and how He shows that love so freely. List specific ways in your daily life you can show Christ's love to others.

SCRIPTURE MEMORIZATION FOR WEEK 4

And, "I will be a Father to you, and you will be my sons and daughters, says the Lord Almighty."

—2 Corinthians 6:18

PRAYER

Dear Father, I so desire to be worthy to be called Your child. Forgive me of my pride. Only with Your hope can I obtain a humble spirit. Only with Your help can I love others as Christ loved me. I need You, Father, every minute of every day. In Jesus' name, amen.

WEEK 5
The Rich Inheritance

DAY 1
Joint Heirs

We know we are going to get what's coming to us—an unbelievable inheritance! We go through exactly what Christ goes through. If we go through the hard times with him, then we're certainly going to go through the good times with him!

—Romans 8:17 *The Message*

Now, in a breathtaking turn, he calls all Christians "heirs of God." This is a miracle, of course, because the heir got the lion's share of the parent's wealth. Paul is saying that what is in store for us is so grand and glorious that it will be, and will feel, as though we each had alone gotten most of the glory of God.

—Timothy Keller, *Romans 8–16 for You*

SERVE EACH OTHER

When our son arrived in the United States, we had many legal details to attend to. I don't remember exactly how long it was after we arrived home, but I remember being jolted by the realization we had another legal process to go through—we needed to change our will to include our son.

Our will paperwork is substantial. We are not wealthy people, but I am married to a detailed Christian man who is cautious, especially about such things as the legal paperwork involved in the preparation of our children's inheritance.

Years later I overheard this very topic come up among our children.

"I would receive the majority of anything Mom and Dad had. I'm the oldest and their biological child. It would only make sense," our daughter proclaimed boldly.

"Don't be silly," our son replied. "I'm the boy. If anyone gets more, it would be me."

First, I was horrified my children would actually have this conversation, let alone say such things to each other. When I addressed their conversation, I let them know their father and I had decided in our will that their inheritance would be equally divided among them.

"I assure you, although this may be hard for you to process now, your biggest inheritance will be your faith and each other," I said. That received their best eye-rolling response. However, that message brought to mind our spiritual inheritance and a similar question about the topic.

In Matthew 20:20–28, the mother of James and John approached Jesus with a bold request. She asked if her sons could be seated beside Him in heaven. Jesus responded that it was God's decision who sat where. However, Jesus did not allow a teachable moment to pass by. "Whoever wants to become great among you must be your servant, and whoever wants to be first must be your slave—just as the Son of Man did not come to be served, but to serve, and to give his life as a ransom for many" (vv. 26–28).

In other words, Jesus suggested that rather than being overly concerned about who is greater and receives a larger portion of the inheritance, we should be more concerned about who can serve each other better. In God's kingdom, we are all coheirs equally, but the greater among us are the ones who desire to become less, not more. We serve and sacrifice for our children, and in doing so, our reward becomes greater. What a great twist, isn't it?

Jesus encouraged us to become humble as He was here on earth. Our servant attitude is key to our inheritance.

1. Thinking about James and John, have you ever thought you should receive a greater portion of something? How has your perspective on that changed, considering Jesus' words in response to the disciples' mother's request?

2. According to Matthew 20:26–28, how do we become great?

3. Read each Scripture listed below and explain in a word or short phrase how each describes our inheritance.

Matthew 25:34

Ephesians 1:18

Hebrews 9:15

OUR UNBELIEVABLE INHERITANCE

I daydream about heaven. I cannot help but wonder what it is like. We hear so much about heaven having streets of gold, but other than that, how much do we really know about it? I wanted to learn more, so I picked up my Bible concordance and looked for verses that pertained to heaven and our spiritual inheritance.

First, I read 1 Peter 1:3–4, "In his great mercy he has given us new birth into a living hope through the resurrection of Jesus Christ from the dead, and into an inheritance that can never perish, spoil or fade. This inheritance is kept in heaven for you."

Although Peter doesn't go into specific details about heaven, he does offer four significant insights into our inheritance: Our inheritance can never expire, our inheritance can never reduce in value, our inheritance can never disappear, and our inheritance is reserved for us in heaven. That is quite the guarantee.

Next, I discovered Revelation 21:4: "'There will be no more death' or mourning or crying or pain, for the old order of things has passed away." Think about that kind of inheritance. We never have to say goodbye to a loved one again. The life here on earth that carries with it so much pain and struggle won't exist there. No sad days, no disease, no bankruptcy, no neglected or abused children.

The thought of those promises overwhelms me. Does it you?

In an article titled "Your Convictions About Heaven," that he wrote for his *In Touch Ministries* blog, Charles Stanley talks about our heavenly inheritance this way, "God didn't put us on this earth to stay here." In the article "More About Heaven: A Place for Us," he emphasizes, "The only thing that will last is our relationship with Christ. And our heavenly treasures are our good deeds, obedience, holiness, and actions of love, kindness, and forgiveness."

Yet I long to know what heaven will *look* like. As I read more, I got the feeling the authors were writing around some secret without actually divulging it. Or is it that maybe they can't? Perhaps our inheritance is so fantastic, they are unable to describe it.

That is when I rediscovered 1 Corinthians 2:9. Referring back to Isaiah 64:4, the Apostle Paul wrote, "As it is written: 'What no eye has seen, what no ear has heard, and what no human mind has conceived'—the things God has prepared for those who love him."

Though not exactly what my heart had been yearning to read, this passage quieted my mind. Heaven is so great, so infinite, that our human minds cannot fathom what God has in store for us. Just the way we, as parents, love to surprise our children on their birthdays or adoption days or Christmas with gifts that overjoy, imagine how much greater our heavenly Father longs to overwhelm us with His goodness and generosity. That's what He promises for His joint heirs.

4. How do we accumulate our heavenly inheritance?

5. As you study about heaven and our inheritance, what aspect is most meaningful to you? Why?

6. According to Ephesians 1:13–14, who is a deposit guaranteeing our inheritance?

7. Read each Scripture below and answer the corresponding question.

   Isaiah 64:4: How is our inheritance described?

   Hebrews 9:15: Our inheritance is both promised and what?

   1 Peter 1:3–5: Our inheritance can never what?

STORING UP OUR INHERITANCE

I admit it. I feel constantly torn between treasure-storing here on earth and treasure-storing in heaven. Can you relate?

At times, I feel so busy serving my husband, my children, my extended family, myself, my etc., that I wonder . . . *how can I fit in one more thing?* How can I earn toward my heavenly bank deposit as well?

That is when the Spirit brings His Word to mind: "Whatever you do, work at it with all your heart, as working for the Lord, not for human masters, since you know that you will receive an inheritance from the Lord as a reward. It is the Lord Christ you are serving" (Colossians 3:23–24).

To think, the Creator of the universe is such a personal God that He would think of our serving others and count it toward our heavenly gain. When we serve our families, we serve Him. As Jesus reminded us, "If anyone gives even a cup of cold water to one of these little ones who is my disciple, truly I tell you, that person will certainly not lose their reward" (Matthew 10:42).

As we go about the business of parenting our children and caring for orphans, God sees and rewards.

> Adoption is not a change in nature, but a change in status. If we fail to see this truth, we will miss the significance of our adoption. . . . Adoption is, instead, a declaration God makes about us. It is irreversible, dependent entirely upon his gracious choice, in which he says: "You are my son, today I have brought you into my family."
>
> —Sinclair B. Ferguson, *Children of the Living God*

8. Reread Colossians 3:23–24. What is our reward for working as for the Lord?

9. Reflect on your heavenly inheritance. Describe everything you
   think of or imagine it to be.

SCRIPTURE MEMORIZATION FOR WEEK 5

Now if we are children, then we are heirs—heirs of God and co-heirs with
Christ, if indeed we share in his sufferings in order that we may also share
in his glory.

—Romans 8:17

PRAYER

Dear Father, You are so magnificent yet so personal. It is hard for me to
comprehend everything You are. When I spend time considering Your
promised inheritance and all things heavenly, my eyes fill with tears and I
am left to my limited human imagination. Help me to live every day thinking of my heavenly impact. In Jesus' name, amen.

DAY 2
Generation to Generation

Giving joyful thanks to the Father, who has qualified you to share in the inheritance of his holy people in the kingdom of light.

—Colossians 1:12

The reason for adopting, in the first-century world, was specifically to have an heir to whom one could bequeath one's goods. So, too, God's adoption of us make us his heirs, and so guarantees to us, as our right (we might say), the inheritance that he has in store for us.

—J. I. Packer, *Knowing God*

GIVING IN THE NOW

When we consider the term *inheritance*, we realize it can be used in the now, as well as in the future. My friend Shelly understands that well.

Shelly enjoys the blessing of both birth and adopted grandchildren. Her daughter Jane attended Moody Bible Institute and, while on a summer break at twenty years old, did mission work in Jamaica. While there, she met a young man named Moses, and for the next twelve years, they wrote, encouraged each other, and stayed connected to each other's lives. Then their relationship shifted, and they decided to marry. After their wedding, Jane agreed to adopt Moses's son and daughter from a former relationship so the children could be raised by their father.

Just as Jane claimed them as her children, Shelly claimed them immediately as her grandchildren. "My grandchildren may have cultural differences," said Shelly, "but their needs to feel loved, secure, accepted, and cared for are all the same."

And as members of her family, she considered them the same heirs in her inheritance. But she doesn't want to wait until she's gone to gift that inheritance out. She learned that lesson through her own experience with her parents. Shelly's parents' will directed a specific division of their property, which the siblings debated, causing a rift between family members. The fracture in family relationships was extremely painful for her.

"I am giving to my children and grandchildren now as well as later. I want them to receive things I see as important and valuable from me now, both physically and spiritually," she said.

When Shelly thinks about the inheritance she wants to provide for her grandchildren, she wants *all* of her grandchildren to know how special and loved they are and that God has given all unique gifts. It isn't just physical things she wants to give. She wants to give the gift of her insight and encouragement so they know who they are and how special they are. "Some of my grandchildren are reserved and quiet. Others are outgoing and rambunctious. I want them to know God created them with unique gifts and abilities. They don't have to try to impress anyone. They are God's children, and He loves them enough to die for them."

Shelly understands that spiritual adoption is about sacrifice and choice. "Jesus made the ultimate sacrifice for us," she said. "He made a choice to die on the Cross. Adoption means sacrifice and choice. I hope to teach my grandchildren to live lives of sacrifice and choice out of their love and gratitude for God." That, to her, would be the best inheritance she could offer them.

Shelly hopes to impress the aspects of daily Christian living on her grandchildren. Whenever they feel life isn't treating them fairly, she reminds them that Jesus said, "In this world you will have trouble. But take heart! I have overcome the world" (John 16:33). She encourages them to try to live out mercy and justice, which begins among their siblings.

"Loving others is always going to mean sacrifice, but sacrifice with grace, and not an attitude," Shelly said. "Modeling integrity and grace is one of the most important gifts I want to leave behind."

One of the verses Shelly prays for her grandchildren is Ephesians 6:7. She inserts their names into the verse and prays they each will develop a servant's heart, serving wholeheartedly as to the Lord and not men.

A grandmother's love is certainly an inheritance to cherish. Especially one steeped in God's love.

1. What spiritual inheritance do you hope to leave your children and/or grandchildren?

2. In Ephesians 6:7–8, we are encouraged to develop a servant's heart, regardless of our station on earth. How does that apply to your life?

3. Read the following Scripture passages and answer how each defines us as heirs.

   Romans 4:13

   Galatians 3:29

   Galatians 4:7

AN INHERITANCE OF GRACE

Considering all the things I shield my children from during the day, I began to wonder, *what inheritance am I leaving behind? How can I leave a powerful spiritual legacy for them?* This is a question for both my mind and my heart. I discovered two ways I am striving to leave a loving inheritance for my children.

First, I am leaving them a lifetime of prayer. I pray for each of my children, remembering specific needs. I used to keep it only in private prayer time but no longer.

I pray for them, in front of them, usually touching their shoulders or head. I want them to remember me praying over them. I want us to celebrate together when God graciously answers these prayers. I pray for their friendships and acceptance among their peers. I pray for healing—physical, mental, and emotional. I pray about their future. I want my prayers poured out to God to reside within them.

When I do not know how to pray for them, I rest in Romans 8:26–27: "In the same way, the Spirit also helps us in our weakness. We do not know what we ought to pray for, but the Spirit himself intercedes for us through wordless groans. And he who searches our hearts knows the mind of the Spirit, because the Spirit intercedes for God's people in accordance with the will of God."

This legacy as a praying mom is the best thing I can offer. I have found it to be an amazing bonding time for us. What started out as awkward has become a time requested by my children. I'm amazed to hear them desire my prayers over them as different issues arise in their lives.

The other inheritance I leave my children is my love of books, especially the Bible. As an avid reader, I have many books, including many versions of the Bible. My children witness me poring over these books. Occasionally, whether they want to hear it or not, they are treated to a selected passage that has encouraged me. They may roll their eyes once and a while, but I believe a love of reading, especially God's Word, is an inherited thing. It brings to mind 2 Timothy 2:15: "Do your best to present yourself to God as one approved, a worker who does not need to be ashamed and who correctly handles the word of truth." That is the kind of legacy I want to leave my children—one of loving God's Word.

The memories of time with my grandmother include her time with the Lord every morning and an unhurried approach to intentional prayer time, usually on our knees together. A lifetime of observing my own mother's devotional and prayer time has impacted me greatly also. As it says in Psalm 145:4, "One generation commends your works to another; they tell of your mighty acts." The inheritance I received from both of these godly women has surely become an inheritance to me. One I gladly pass to the next generation.

4. In what ways can you leave a legacy of prayer and time in God's Word?

5. Why do you think that's important?

6. How else can parents leave a legacy of love of God for their children?

7. Read each of the following Scripture passages and answer the corresponding question.

   Luke 12:32: What does our Father give us?

   Luke 22:28–29: Who has God given the kingdom to?

   Acts 20:32: Who receives the inheritance?

A JOYFUL INHERITANCE

There never seems to be enough time. I find myself longing for more time with each of my children to make them feel special and loved.

Keeping enough time in the day has been a challenge I have willingly taken on. I am trying to be deliberate about making time for those I love. I have found the only way to have the time I need is by intentionally creating white space on my overcrowded calendar. I'm the kind of parent who needs to plan time with my kids. Especially for joyful family times.

When my children reminisce about our family, it is my prayer they remember being joyful together, feeling loved and special, just as they are to our Father.

A good person leaves an inheritance for their children's children.

—Proverbs 13:22

8. Reflect on how you want to be remembered by each of your children. Make a list so you can access and remember it.

SCRIPTURE MEMORIZATION FOR WEEK 5

Now if we are children, then we are heirs—heirs of God and co-heirs with Christ, if indeed we share in his sufferings in order that we may also share in his glory.

—Romans 8:17

PRAYER

Dear Father, thank You for Your loving ways. Thank You for an inheritance far beyond what I deserve. Help me to be mindful of the inheritance I leave my children on earth and toward heaven. Encourage my heart today with heavenly imaginings. In Jesus' name, amen.

DAY 3

The Importance of Our Vulnerability

Jesus said, "Let the little children come to me, and do not hinder them, for the kingdom of heaven belongs to such as these."

—Matthew 19:14

This is all the inheritance I give to my dear family. The religion of Christ will give them one which will make them rich indeed.

—Patrick Henry, from his will, cited in *The True Patrick Henry* by George Morgan

THE RIGHT THING TO DO

Adoption changes a child's life in many ways. A family offers security, nurture, and stability. Family can also offer life, here on earth, as well as a heavenly inheritance. This is true in Kathy's adoption story.

It all began with a mission trip Kathy's mom took to Albania. She met a young girl named Annabelle, who had beta thalassemia, a genetic blood disorder that prevents the body from being able to produce healthy red blood cells.

When Kathy's mom returned from Albania, she couldn't get young Annabelle out of her mind, and she told Kathy about the girl and her desperate need for a family and medical treatment. At the time, Kathy and her husband had four children, so while Kathy listened with sympathy, she wasn't prepared to do anything about the Albanian girl. Their third child Alan, however, was. He seemed particularly affected by Annabelle's troubles, and began encouraging his parents to consider adopting the girl.

"Alan persisted in our adopting this young girl," Kathy told me. "He was our most materialistic child, and even as a seven-year-old, he took very good care of his things. When he told us he was willing to sell all his toys if it would help us adopt Annabelle, we knew we needed to take the next step."

Kathy decided to send a photo of their family to the adoption agency connected with Annabelle's orphanage. In response, they learned she had a grandmother who visited her once a month and that she was not available for adoption. Kathy thought that was the end of it.

Months later, the director of the orphanage showed the family photo to Annabelle's grandmother. Annabelle's grandmother loved her very much, and because she wanted the best for her granddaughter, she approved Annabelle's adoption to Kathy's family.

Then Kathy found out how much the adoption would cost.

"It was more than my husband made in a year!" she said. "I could see no possible way for us to adopt her." But the thought of adopting never left her mind.

"Adoption was more about being there for a child who desperately needed us, and less about adding another member to our already-large family," Kathy said. It became a mission.

As word got out that Kathy and her family wanted to adopt this child, some people wanted to help. One couple from Pennsylvania heard their story and sent a personal check for $1,250 toward the adoption expenses.

Twelve months later, they were able to adopt Annabelle and she was able to receive immediate medical treatment. Kathy's family went on to adopt two more girls from China with the same diagnosis. Kathy continues to advocate adoption for other children with beta thalassemia.

"It just seems the right thing to do," Kathy said. "Our girls are thriving with the love of a family and excellent medical care. They have hope where they once had none."

Annabelle's adopting family made themselves vulnerable through their willingness to open their hearts and home to her. This type of vulnerability, this openness and trust in our heavenly Father, is another way we inherit the kingdom of heaven.

1. Read Psalm 121:1–2. Where does our help ultimately come from?

2. Read each Scripture passage and consider how each describes our becoming vulnerable.

   Proverbs 14:30

   2 Corinthians 4:7

   James 1:2

3. Read Mark 9:33–37 and Mark 10:13–16. Summarize what these passages mean in light of being vulnerable in our utter dependence on God.

VULNERABLE AS A CHILD

Our inheritance depends upon our ability to become vulnerable to God as our only source. In order to receive the gift of heaven, Jesus instructs us to become as vulnerable and dependent upon our heavenly Father as a child (see Matthew 19:14). It is not the childish characteristic we are to assume; it is the recognition of our vulnerability, our openness, and utter, daily need of Him. Just as Anabelle was dependent upon her new family for medical help, we are to be dependent upon God, trusting that He will care for us and will make a way when we see none.

Our vulnerability makes us more Christlike in three important ways.

First, it leads to our dying to our human nature. Appearing vulnerable is often in direct contrast to what we naturally want to do. We would rather hide our weakness and vulnerability than display or admit them. However, only by admitting our vulnerability can we allow God to show us who He is. Paul talked about this in his second letter to the believers in Corinth:

He said to me, "My grace is sufficient for you, for my power is made perfect in weakness." Therefore, I will boast all the more gladly about my weaknesses, so that Christ's power may rest on me. That is why, for Christ's sake, I delight in weaknesses, in insults, in hardships, in persecutions, in difficulties. For when I am weak, then I am strong.

—2 Corinthians 12:9–10

Second, it leads to our loving others as Christ loved us. By becoming vulnerable to others, our serving them becomes less constricted by what others think. In this way, we imitate what Christ did for us, as we see in Philippians 2:5–7, "In your relationships with one another, have the same mindset as Christ Jesus: Who, being in very nature God, did not consider equality with God something to be used to his own advantage; rather, he made himself nothing by taking the very nature of a servant, being made in human likeness." Loving and serving others, regardless of who we think we are, humbles us and opens us to our need of God.

Third, our vulnerability keeps us focused on God. Just as Jesus was totally dependent on God during His ministry on earth, so we are also to take everything to God. As we become vulnerable, He becomes our everything. We become less; He becomes more. Our need for Him becomes so great, we seek Him out throughout the day, sneaking away to pray. The Gospels are full of references to the amount of time Jesus spent in prayer with God, displaying His utter need of His Father. We can find Him praying in multiple passages, including these.

"After He had dismissed the crowds, He went up on the mountain by Himself to pray. When it was evening, He was there alone" (Matthew 14:23 AMP).

"Very early in the morning, while it was still dark, Jesus got up, left the house and went off to a solitary place, where he prayed" (Mark 1:35).

By our becoming vulnerable and open to our need of God the Father, we become more Christlike. As we embrace the world's vulnerable children, we reach beyond our own human nature and display God's concern for all. As we care, displaying God's goodness for the orphan, we are then able to grant all glory and praise to God and receive our inheritance with Christ.

4. In Mark 9:33–37 and Mark 10:13–16, what was Jesus trying to teach His disciples?

5. Read each Scripture passage and answer the corresponding question.

2 Corinthians 4:7: Our power belongs to whom?

2 Corinthians 12:9–10: Why are we to delight in our weakness?

Galatians 6:2: How are we to be vulnerable to one another?

TRUST COMPLETELY

For many people the idea of vulnerability brings negative connotations. After all, many believe that to be vulnerable means to be weak, powerless, exposed, and defenseless.

Is that what God wants us to be like?

Surprisingly, I found a great biblical definition of *vulnerable* in an unlikely source—UrbanDictionary.com. This is how they defined the word: "Someone who is completely and rawly open, unguarded with their *heart, mind, and soul*. Being vulnerable happens when you *trust completely*" (emphasis added).

Reading the words *heart, mind, and soul* reminds me of Matthew 22:37–39. A man came to Jesus and asked Him what the greatest commandment was. Jesus replied that we are to "'love the Lord your God with all your heart and with all your soul and with all your mind.' This is the first and greatest commandment. And the second is like it: 'Love your neighbor as yourself.'" In other words, if you sift it down to its basest form, Jesus is calling us to be vulnerable. To love vulnerably. Our becoming vulnerable as a child opens our ability to be totally open with God, with all our heart, mind, and soul.

Becoming vulnerable to God means we trust Him completely. The inverse also holds true: when we trust completely, we become vulnerable to the One we trust.

Vulnerability is the birthplace of love, belonging, joy, courage, empathy, and creativity. It is the source of hope, empathy, accountability, and authenticity. If we want greater clarity in our purpose or deeper and more meaningful spiritual lives, vulnerability is the path.

—Brené Brown, *Daring Greatly: How the Courage to Be Vulnerable Transforms the Way We Live, Love, Parent, and Lead*

6. How does Matthew 22:37–39 relate to our being vulnerable or open to God?

7. Reflect on the ways your adoption journey made you more vulnerable to God.

SCRIPTURE MEMORIZATION FOR WEEK 5

Now if we are children, then we are heirs—heirs of God and co-heirs with Christ, if indeed we share in his sufferings in order that we may also share in his glory.

—Romans 8:17

PRAYER

Dear Father, thank You for loving me as Your child. I am constantly overwhelmed by Your love and patience with me. May Your words reside in my mind, heart, and soul. Thank You for the incredible gift of inheritance through Jesus Christ, Your Son. In Jesus' name, amen.

DAY 4
Living Inheritance

May the God of hope fill you with all joy and peace as you trust in him, so that you may overflow with hope by the power of the Holy Spirit.

—Romans 15:13

It is a celebration of the fact that we were adopted for a purpose and that adoption is an experience that has the potential of teaching us some of life's richest and deepest lessons.

—Sherrie Eldridge, *Twenty Life-Transforming Choices Adoptees Need to Make*

SPECIAL NEEDS ADOPTION

The special needs adoption journey can be difficult. We give up things we treasure, like large amounts of our time or our own personal comfort, in order to give more attention to the needs our children have. Sometimes that sacrifice comes with hidden blessings we could easily miss. The beauty of our heavenly inheritance is that we don't have to wait to enjoy it. If we train our eyes and hearts to the things of God, we can find God's blessings here right now.

"It's like a secret treasure," my friend, Tammy, told me.

I had met Tammy and her husband Jay a couple times, mainly through school events. Our children are in the same grade and class at school. Their family consisted of three boys—Riley, Charlie, and Joseph—before they adopted Maria and Sigita.

"Within minutes of meeting them, our boys put a different face on special needs adoption," she said. "They wouldn't be the boys they are without our adopting. And to think, people in our lives actually worried about our adopting special needs children . . . it makes me laugh."

That's the secret treasure Tammy is referring to. Many people shy away from adopting special needs children—some of the most vulnerable children—because they fear it will be too much work. As though the cons outweigh the pros. But Tammy and her family have found the opposite to be true. Is it difficult work? Yes, Tammy says. But the work bears blessings because of how it changes their family to become more Christlike.

The real joy comes when others take notice. Tammy had the girls in a restaurant recently, which comes with its own set of challenges. During their meal, a woman who was leaving the restaurant walked by Tammy and said, "You're a good mom. I was a special needs teacher for many years, and you're a good mom."

"Isn't that just like the Holy Spirit to speak to my doubts through a total stranger at Wendy's?" Tammy said.

God presented Tammy and her husband an opportunity to serve as parents and to adopt children with special needs. They obeyed. "Now it's as if our gift of salvation has been made all the sweeter for it," Tammy said. "I don't know if our heavenly inheritance will look any different, but my living inheritance here on earth has been made better because of it."

God loves to give gifts to His children. Isn't it just like Him to call Tammy and her family to something as challenging as special needs adoption, only to have it be such a blessing to them? God only wants what is best for us. Just as Jesus said in John 14:23, "Anyone who loves me will obey my teaching. My Father will love them, and we will come to them and make our home with them."

It's counterintuitive, but here's the truth: serving God by serving others is part of our inheritance here on earth. When we give of ourselves as Christ commands, we receive joy. What an inheritance to experience then *and* now.

1. Read John 14:23 and restate it in your own words.

2. How can trusting God help in our obedience?

3. Read the following Scripture passages, and answer how each passage describes trusting God.

Exodus 15:2

Isaiah 41:10

1 Corinthians 2:4–5

WHAT IS YOUR IDOL?

In Matthew 19:16–22, we read about a rich young man of nobility who approached Jesus with an interesting question. He wanted an assurance of eternal life. "What good thing must I do to get eternal life?" (v. 16). Jesus answered him in three ways.

First, Jesus directed the young man toward the true meaning of good, in that only God was truly good (v. 17). Second, Jesus spoke of the law, namely the commandments in verses 18 and 19, "'You shall not murder, you shall not commit adultery, you shall not steal, you shall not give false testimony, honor your father and mother,' and 'love your neighbor as yourself.'" The young man agreed by saying he kept those. Then he asked Jesus what he lacked.

That is when Jesus answered him the third and final time. Jesus directed him to sell everything he had and to give it to the poor, ensuring his heavenly inheritance. Jesus also invited the young man to join Him, presumably as a disciple (v. 21).

Sadly, the man left, discouraged by Jesus' words and unwilling to give for the greater good of an eternal inheritance.

I struggle with the young man's reluctance. He was invited to follow Jesus, to walk with Him daily, to actively engage in ministry with Him, and to see, firsthand, Jesus' miracles. Yet he was unable to let go of his wealth, so he turned and walked away. This has to be one of the saddest stories in the Bible.

Jesus used it as a spiritual lesson for all of us. For this young man, wealth had become his security, what he trusted, and his idol. We want our security to be God, to trust in God alone.

How do we know if we have an idol in our lives? I heard one pastor explain it this way: "You don't know what idols you worship until Jesus says, 'I want it.'"

Those idols keep us from pursuing the greater wealth—our spiritual inheritance.

For me, wealth isn't an idol. However, I may have another idol that I value greatly: my comfort. I am especially reminded of this every time I camp. I enjoy my comfortable mattress and pillow, and things like clean water and air conditioning. I wanted our adoption to be comfortable also. It makes me wonder, have I truly died to self with my craving of comfort?

In speaking with others regarding orphan care and adoption, the topic of comfort often arises. We speak of it in other terms, though, of course.

"We couldn't possibly handle any more children."

"We are so close to retirement, we wouldn't make good foster parents at this stage of our lives."

How often do those seemingly innocent idols get in the way of following Jesus as He calls us to do? To leave our comfort and follow Him into desperate places where hopeless children need hope. How often have we, like the rich young man, sadly shaken our heads and walked away from Jesus and our inheritance?

We must take our idols and hold them up against what Jesus said in Matthew 6:33, "Seek first his kingdom and his righteousness, and all these things will be given to you as well." All the inheritance *God* has planned for us.

4. After reading Matthew 19:16–22, what part of the conversation between Jesus and the rich young man stood out most to you and why?

5. Do you have any idols preventing you from ministry opportunities? How can you take one step closer to obedience in that area?

6. Read each Scripture passage and answer the corresponding question.

   Proverbs 10:28: What can the righteous expect?

   James 1:2–3: What are we to consider pure joy?

   1 Peter 1:6: We should rejoice now, even though we may suffer what?

FINDING JOY IN MISSION

God, through His Spirit, brings a deep, satisfying joy that keeps us grounded while we are still pressing on to our ultimate heavenly inheritance. As the writer of Hebrews reminded us, "Through Jesus, therefore, let us continually offer to God a sacrifice of praise—the fruit of lips that openly profess his name. And do not forget to do good and to share with others, for with such sacrifices God is pleased" (Hebrews 13:15–16).

> Adoption and orphan care is a joyful and unpredictable adventure.
>
> —Tony Merida, *Ordinary: How to Turn the World Upside Down*

7. According to Hebrews 13:15–16, what sacrifices are pleasing to God?

8. Reflect on and write about the ways adoption, even in the areas of struggle, has brought you joy.

9. How can serving God through serving others bring us a living inheritance here on earth?

SCRIPTURE MEMORIZATION FOR WEEK 5

Now if we are children, then we are heirs—heirs of God and co-heirs with Christ, if indeed we share in his sufferings in order that we may also share in his glory.

—Romans 8:17

PRAYER

Dear Father, You are my source of joy. Thank You for Your Holy Spirit that helps me find the gift of Your joy in my work for You. You are so gracious to me, Father. May Your joy overflow from me to my family and community. In Jesus' name, amen.

DAY 5
Living in One World

We fix our eyes not on what is seen, but on what is unseen, since what is seen is temporary, but what is unseen is eternal.

—2 Corinthians 4:18

You have stories worth telling, memories worth remembering, dreams worth working toward, a body worth feeding, a soul worth tending, and beyond that, the God of the universe dwells within you, the true culmination of super and natural. You are more than dust and bones. You are spirit and power and image of God. And you have been given Today.

—Shauna Niequist, *Cold Tangerines: Celebrating the Extraordinary Nature of Everyday Life*

THE DISCOURAGEMENT OF HEARTBREAK

After Svetlana's tuberculosis testing, she didn't have to say a word. I knew by looking at her she had tested positive.

"It is worse than I could have imagined," she told me. "It is a type of TB that will be difficult to fight. I already have pustules in my right lung. They told me I should have it removed."

I was stunned.

"I will have to go through more testing to make sure my body is healthy enough for the operation," she continued. "I think I will need to go to Kiev for this."

I had time in Ukraine to take additional steps for Svetlana's care. I called friends who lived and worked in the greater Odessa area. They were willing to help her get into the tuberculosis hospital in Kiev.

Meanwhile, I interviewed a healthcare worker from the city. Her name was Svetlana also. She worked as a social worker with an HIV prevention center in Odessa. She was willing to take on Svetlana part-time as a personal client. She also spoke English, which greatly aided our communication.

This is the way we built family around Svetlana for the next few years. I saved every dollar I could to send to her in Ukraine. She tried to continue her trade school classes, also receiving limited education funds from the government, but eventually had to drop out, ending any stipend the government offered.

She got settled in Kiev for treatment. After about two weeks, against my wishes, she walked out of the hospital and returned to Odessa. This type of behavior would soon become routine. Like most children from orphanages, she had a huge chip on her shoulder. If she didn't like a doctor or hospital roommate, she would check herself out and leave the treatment program—even if someone had worked for weeks to get her into that treatment center. It was frustrating for everyone concerned. She was an adult now and half a world away from me in Ukraine. I felt helpless.

It seemed hard for Svetlana to believe her tuberculosis was life-threatening, regardless of what anyone told her. She ended up in a small apartment and continued to try to have a life, like her friends. I kept warning her that she was highly contagious and that she must take good care of her health. I am not sure my concern was persuasive.

Her next call, months later, sent me to my knees.

"Kim, they have found tuberculosis in my organs . . . and in my brain," Svetlana said.

I continued to pray for God's guidance. I contacted everyone I knew who knew anything about tuberculosis, including a doctor friend from church, our county health department, and an acquaintance who worked in the Centers for Disease Control and Prevention (CDC). It turns out Ukraine, as well as other Eastern European countries, are known for a particular strain of multidrug-resistant tuberculosis (MDR TB).

I tried to keep her spirits up. A doctor friend, Dr. Oleg Guzik, who also pastored a Baptist church in Yuzhny, Ukraine (approximately thirty miles, but an hour's travel time from where Svetlana was hospitalized), traveled to Odessa to speak with her, at my request. She prayed with him and confessed her sins. Dr. Guzik was very kind to visit her. He contacted me with the news. He also expressed his concern for her.

The next call I received was to let me know Svetlana had died, a few months before her twenty-second birthday.

When we encounter a struggle in our adoption or family, how we keep striving in our Christian life can have a powerful effect on both our own hearts as well as on others. Satan uses any discouragement to attack our peace. First Peter 5:7–8, reminds us, "Cast all your anxiety on him because he cares for you. Be alert and of sober mind. Your enemy the devil prowls around like a roaring lion looking for someone to devour." We must keep on guard and not grow weary of doing what we know is right—even when everything we see around us seems that we are defeated.

1. Read 2 Corinthians 4:18 listed at the beginning of today's study. Rephrase it in your own words.

2. In 1 Peter 5:7–8, how are we to remain focused on God and our heavenly inheritance?

3. Look up the following Scripture passages and answer how each passage describes where our focus should be.

   Matthew 6:33

   Romans 8:5

Colossians 3:2

WHERE IS MY FOCUS?

In Philippians 3, we read about how we are to be confident in our faith through the Spirit within us and not confident in our flesh. We are encouraged to forget the past and to continue to strive toward the goal of heaven.

Keeping focused on our heavenly goal can be difficult. Sometimes, it's the stress we face in everyday life that steals our attention away. At other times, it can be the influence of someone or something unholy in our lives. Or we struggle while helping our children deal with trauma.

Paul encourages us to keep focused on our heavenly goal, our inheritance. No matter what may come our way as Christians, we are to remember to keep our focus on Christ.

Whenever life seems to be going sideways instead of forward, it can appear impossible to keep the goal of unification with Christ and collection of our inheritance in the forefront of our minds. Our spiritual journey is not complete yet, so how do we possibly move forward after such a [insert your recent disappointment here]?

In Philippians 3:12–14, Paul defines three ways for us to stay focused.

In verse 12, it reads, "Not that I have already obtained all this, or have already arrived at my goal, but I press on to take hold of that for which Christ Jesus took hold of me." He encourages us to focus on God and what he has done for us. He has a plan for our life. He doesn't want us to miss any of it.

Verse 13 tells us, "I do not consider myself yet to have taken hold of it. But one thing I do: Forgetting what is behind and straining toward what is ahead." We are encouraged not to look back. This applies not only to past mistakes but past successes as well. We are to stay present in our focus.

Then Paul summed it up in verse 14: "I press on toward the goal to win the prize for which God has called me heavenward in Christ Jesus." We are to stretch out toward our heavenly goal, as a runner extends toward the finish line in a race. We are to press on, keeping our eyes heaven focused. Our spiritual growth depends on it.

After Svetlana's death, I felt empty. The five years she had been in our lives had been full of pain and separation, but the years had also brought smiles and determination. Ultimately, I had to keep focused on seeing her again one day. I kept focused on her younger brother, our son, in our present. I stretched out my faith toward heaven, pleading for comfort when the tears would come.

The adoption journey will have its days of joy and challenges. By staying focused on the present and striving toward our ultimate goal of Christlikeness and heaven, we can win the race that Paul referred to. Keeping focused on the eternal keeps us close to God, which is exactly where we want to be.

4. How do you keep heavenly focused?

5. Where does a child of God find comfort?

6. Read each of the following Scripture passages and answer the corresponding question.

   Romans 6:23: How does Paul describe eternal life?

   1 Timothy 6:12: When do we take hold of our eternal life?

James 1:2–4: Why should we be joyful when we face trials?

THAT'S WHAT HAPPENS . . .

As I was thinking about everything that had happened, I recalled something a friend mentioned to me a couple years before Svetlana's death. We were discussing the importance of caring for vulnerable children.

"That's what happens when children aren't in families, Kim. Orphans die," she said. Like most, I didn't think I would ever experience it firsthand. Yet even in death, Svetlana continued to teach me.

I learned why God cares so much for the vulnerable. His creation is completely vulnerable without Him. Especially the children. We are often the only chance the vulnerable will ever have to know love, emotionally and spiritually. He instructs us to love them as He loves us in order that, through our service to Him, we will understand how He much loves and cares for us.

I learned orphan care is serious ministry. While it isn't always recognized or represented as a ministry in some churches, I know firsthand the heartbreak of working with the orphaned. I have witnessed the suffering. I know the pain. It is to be entered into with much prayer and with godly people beside you.

I learned how intimately I am loved. I know this level of love because I experience it every day in our home. I know the overwhelming quality of love I have for both our son and daughter. Considering who God is lets me know how much infinitely more He must love me, His adopted child.

If every Christian could experience this love for a child born of another woman, our world would be a changed place. If every Christian understood on such a personal level how much they are loved, we would radically affect everything and everyone around us. All due to our undeserved adoption and the incredible inheritance it includes, both here on earth and in heaven.

In the New Testament, we don't find our gift through self-examination and introspection and then find ways to express it. Instead we love one another, serve one another, help one another, and in so doing we see how God has equipped us to do so.

—Russell D. Moore, *Adopted for Life: The Priority of Adoption for Christian Families and Churches*

SCRIPTURE MEMORIZATION FOR WEEK 5

Now if we are children, then we are heirs—heirs of God and co-heirs with Christ, if indeed we share in his sufferings in order that we may also share in his glory.

—Romans 8:17

PRAYER

Dear Father, thank You for being a father to the fatherless. Thank You for Your encouragement to love others the way You love us. I see You in the many small ways You are working in the lives of adoptive families today. I pray the church around the world will strive to shepherd the vulnerable. In Jesus' name, amen.

WEEK 6

The Ministry of Orphan Care

DAY 1

Adoption and Caring for the Fatherless

Pure and unblemished religion [as it is expressed in outward acts] in the sight of our God and Father is this: to visit and look after the fatherless and the widows in their distress, and to keep oneself uncontaminated by the [secular] world.

—James 1:27 AMP

It is not as if I—or the church as a whole—was hard-hearted and didn't care about the plight of orphans. I simply did not know the enormity of the problems. No one had seriously engaged the issue of orphan care in any of the churches or schools I attended. But in this case, ignorance is not bliss. Millions of kids around the world are hurting in ways we cannot imagine, and we are called to respond with compassionate care.

—Johnny Carr, *Orphan Justice: How to Care for Orphans Beyond Adopting*

GOD'S MANDATE TO CARE

Most adoptive parents have been dramatically affected by their adoptions or other forms of caring for vulnerable children and often become the best advocates for adoption and orphan care. Their advocacy takes form in helping their churches and communities become more aware and open to children's needs. They can also help shape state and national legislation, share their stories through the media, and create new or expand existing orphan care ministries.

When we think of the greater umbrella of orphan care ministry, adoptive parents are the best experienced to explain why adoption is a crucial part of orphan care. We can explain why not every child in an institution or described as orphaned is available for such immersive care as adoption (due to existing family who are unable to care for the child but also who do not wish to relinquish their rights). That is why we use the broader term of orphan care. It encompasses caring for the fatherless in its many forms.

Throughout the Bible we can see God's care and concern for orphans. Starting in the Old Testament, He makes His directives clear. We read in such passages as Deuteronomy 10:18; Psalm 10:14; and Psalm 82:3, among many others, that it is our duty as His children to seek after the welfare of the orphaned (the widowed, and the foreigner).

The early church, those who actually walked with Christ, were also concerned about orphan care. We can read in Matthew 18:5; Matthew 25:45; and James 1:27 how the New Testament writers encouraged us to continue living out God's commands.

Historians confirm what we read in the Bible. One example is of German theologian Gerhard Uhlhorn who described the early church's care of orphans in his book *Christian Charity in the Ancient Church*:

> When we first meet the mention of the adoption and bringing up of foundlings, this work appears not as a novelty, but as one long practised. It is true that the heathen also used to take care of exposed children, but for the purpose of bringing them up as gladiators or prostitutes, or to use them in their own service. . . . Christians brought up the children whom they took charge of for the Lord, and for a respectable and industrious life.

Perhaps the beautiful part of both biblical and secular history is that we continue to see Christians obeying God's commands to care for the fatherless today.

1. Explain in your own words why God is so concerned about orphans and why He asks us to care for them.

2. How did the early church regard orphan care?

3. Read the following Scripture passages and consider how God is referred to in each passage.

Deuteronomy 10:18

Psalm 10:14

Psalm 68:5

PURE RELIGION

One of the things I love about the Apostle James is that he sees the clear responsibility between our redemption and then working out our salvation because of our deep gratitude and love for God. His entire book focuses on the idea that if we have only faith and don't actively pursue growing God's kingdom, then our faith is worthless and dead (see James 2:14–26).

Before he hits us with that moving reality, he spends some time talking about our faith and what constitutes pure religion (see James 1:19–27). In particular, James 1:27 (AMP) gets to the heart of our concern: "Pure and unblemished religion [as it is expressed in outward acts] in the sight of our God and Father is this: to visit and look after the fatherless and the widows in their distress, and to keep oneself uncontaminated by the [secular] world."

We have probably read this verse multiple times, but rather than just assume you and I "get" it, let's spend some time breaking this verse down into bite-sized phrases. I'm borrowing some of these ideas from the brilliant *InterVarsity Press New Testament Commentary Series*, which does an amazing job of helping us understand what James's words meant to the church in that culture and how they apply to the church in today's culture as well.

Pure and unblemished religion in the sight of our God and Father is this. When James defines our outward act of religion, how we live it out, he is careful to describe it as untainted and without fault, as if we are walking out our faith in front God Himself, that He is our ever-present witness. A good reminder!

To visit and look after.
James wants us to know if we desire to remain in that pure and unblemished state, then we must do two things in particular (with the orphaned and widowed): spend time with and take care of them. If we want to stay pure in the eyes of God (our own personal purity), then we must be vigilant in our concern for loving the vulnerable (visit and look after). To James, you cannot be one without the other.

The fatherless and the widows.
James is clear about who specifically we are to visit and care for: those who are vulnerable and unable to care for themselves. Of course, looking after orphans and widows was nothing new for the church. Even those who had not been raised in the church had heard of the Christians' work among the orphaned and widowed. James understood that these two groups of people, in particular, are near and dear to God's heart.

In their distress.
This phrase "refers literally to a pressing or a pressure, or figuratively to an affliction or oppression." Just as they were then, the plight of the orphan (or neglected child) and widow (or elderly persons), as well as the poor and foreigner, are still regarded as oppressed peoples. The prophet Isaiah's words still ring true today: "Learn to do right; seek justice. Defend the oppressed. Take up the cause of the fatherless; plead the case of the widow" (Isaiah 1:17).

It's clear James considers helping those in need, especially those not in a position to help themselves, as an example of living out one's faith before God and others. In our pursuit of pure religion, we must take seriously the call and responsibility to look after or shepherd those who cannot help themselves. We please our Father when we do.

4. As you consider James 1:27 and how the apostle described pure religion, how does it influence your thinking about orphan care?

5. Does James 1:27 still apply to the church today? Why or why not?

6. Read each Scripture passage below and answer the corresponding question.

   Exodus 22:21–23: How will God react if the widow or fatherless cry out to Him?

   Proverbs 31:8–9: Who are we to speak up for?

   Malachi 3:5: How does God say He will act against those who oppose the widows and fatherless?

PAST EXPERIENCE

My corporate career was in the human resources field. One thing I looked for while recruiting was the past experience of the potential candidate. Past experience often spoke louder to me than anything else as an indicator of future performance.

I believe the same is true for us today as we work in the area of orphan care. By understanding the past, through God's grace, we can help shape the future of the church's role. By studying the past, we can determine what has worked and what hasn't.

By bringing hearts and minds together, within our churches, communities, and faith, we can collectively ask God to help us reach out effectively to those he has remained committed to. The church remains the best way for us to reach the orphan (as well as the widow, foreigner, and disadvantaged). Studying God's Word and learning what the early church workers believed, as well as where God is presently leading us, can only encourage His great love through us.

And then, all that's left to take is the appropriate action.

Who better than those who have already taken the adoption journey? Who better than you and me?

> We learned that orphans are easier to ignore before you know their names. They are easier to ignore before you see their faces. It is easier to pretend they're not real before you hold them in your arms. But once you do, everything changes.
>
> —David Platt, *Radical: Taking Back Your Faith from the American Dream*

7. Have you ever thought about the ways you could continue reaching out to orphans? What, if anything, has stopped you?

8. Reflect on James 1:27. Write how it applies to the church today.

SCRIPTURE MEMORIZATION FOR WEEK 6

Religion that God our Father accepts as pure and faultless is this: to look after orphans and widows in their distress and to keep oneself from being polluted by the world.

—James 1:27

PRAYER

Dear Father, thank You for loving me and others as Your children. Thank You for allowing me to be Your loving arms to the needy and loveless of this world. Use me to draw others to You and Your ways. In Jesus' name, amen.

DAY 2

Reaching Aging-Out Foster Youth

Defend the weak and the fatherless; uphold the cause of the poor and the oppressed. Rescue the weak and the needy; deliver them from the hand of the wicked.

—Psalm 82:3–4

Loving a wounded child into wholeness is the most difficult, yet the most significant and rewarding, work anyone can do.

—Rhonda Sciortino, introduction of *Faith and Foster Care: How We Impact God's Kingdom* by John DeGarmo

TRANSITIONAL CARE

Rick first recognized the need of aging-out foster youth (those young people who have turned eighteen and no longer qualify for state-assisted housing through foster care) through his wife Lisa and her involvement as a Court Appointed Special Advocate (CASA). According to their website, "CASA volunteers are appointed by judges to watch over and advocate for abused and neglected children, to make sure they don't get lost in the overburdened legal and social service system or languish in inappropriate group or foster homes." Lisa and Rick saw dozens of teenagers who were becoming adults—aging out—and were then turned out of the Michigan foster care system with no one they could trust.

"I remember a young person was being taken to the homeless mission on their eighteenth birthday because there was no place else for them to go," Rick told me. "I went to the Department of Human Services (DHS) and asked them why."

Rick was told there were few options for young people after foster care. They could go to college. They could try to find independent living with a meager rent subsidy. Or they could go to the mission. Feeling discouraged that these kids were essentially being pushed out and forgotten forced him to his knees in prayer.

Not long after, Rick heard a message at his church that talked about the importance of living out love. As he listened, his mind went to how he could help those aging-out kids. He had to do something.

"After I confirmed there really was a need, I tried to talk to others about it. No one seemed to want to join me," Rick said. "Yet I still felt the burden. I decided to buy a house. It was an *If you build it, they will come* approach, I guess." Lakeshore Lifeworks Ministries (LLM) had begun.

Rick connected to the DHS office in his county. They helped him navigate the complex situation of transitioning youth out of foster care. They were his first big connection to moving forward with the vision God had given him.

Next, Rick connected to his church, which offers assistance to support layperson-led ministries. His church helped him learn how to operate as a ministry. They offered leadership counseling, helped develop a leadership structure, and guided him as he put together a nonprofit board of directors.

LLM offers former foster care kids—boys between the ages eighteen and twenty-one—shared housing in the countryside. Permanent house parents live onsite and help the residents learn how to develop time management skills, eat healthy, and hone leadership skills. Residents acquire personal care, proper hygiene, and driver's license training, learn money management and budgeting skills, obtain employment training and educational support, gain spiritual and emotional health, learn the value of community service, and develop as young people of integrity.

"I remember one young man who was resistant to everything we tried to do for him," Rick said. "A pastor, the house parents, a volunteer, and I all prayed earnestly and specifically for this young man. He was different after that. He didn't isolate himself anymore. He engaged with others and opened up. It was a new beginning, a new life for him."

Rick has been amazed by how he's seen God show up in this ministry. "My prayer life has been affected most since God started this ministry through me," said Rick. "Prayer brings Him among us. He responds. Not always as I ask Him to but in a clear way."

That is exactly what God intends for His people. Our loving children where they are brings glory to God, and it begins with prayer.

1. Read Psalm 82:3–4. In what ways does it apply to the aging-out foster youth of today?

2. What part of Lakeshore Lifeworks Ministries' development stood out to you? Why?

3. Read the following Scripture passages and answer how each applies to foster youth ministry.

   Proverbs 3:27

   Galatians 6:2

   Hebrews 6:10

PRAYER FROM GOD'S PERSPECTIVE

Hearing how important prayer was to Rick's ministry reminds me of prayer's significance, not only in my ministry efforts, but with my relationship with my Father. We need to keep prayer at the forefront of everything we do. And what better example do we have of that than of Jesus?

Reading through the Gospels recently, I was struck by how often Jesus was in prayer. He went to the mountains to pray, He went alone to pray, He looked up toward heaven and prayed, and on and on. Even the disciples asked Jesus how to pray, so they must have recognized the importance of prayer in Jesus' life. It's easy to see that prayer is significant, since Jesus practiced it so often. But it raises another question: *What does God desire from our prayer time with him?*

God desires prayer to be necessary.
Our prayer time with Him shows our dependency on Him. It is a time of bowing down before Him in submission. It acknowledges our complete inadequacy in ourselves and our complete dependence on Him. As our relationship with Him grows, our need to take all things to Him in prayer also increases. It becomes a natural and necessary part of our daily lives.

In John 15:4–5, Jesus said, "Remain in me, as I also remain in you. No branch can bear fruit by itself; it must remain in the vine. Neither can you bear fruit unless you remain in me. I am the vine; you are the branches. If you remain in me and I in you, you will bear much fruit; apart from me you can do nothing."

When we pray, we recognize that our lives are part of the Vine, and He gives us strength and nourishment.

God desires prayer to be yielding.
Our time with Him in prayer is to consistently show we have died to ourselves and now desire only His will for our lives. In this we can claim God's promises. In this the weak are made strong. In this all glory is God's alone. In this Galatians 2:20 becomes true of us: "I have been crucified with Christ and I no longer live, but Christ lives in me. The life I now live in the body, I live by faith in the Son of God, who loved me and gave himself for me."

God desires prayer to be relational.
Jesus taught His disciples to pray to God as Father. Being able to address God as our Father shows the intimacy of our relationship. It causes us to be ever mindful of the fact that He adopted us and regards us as His children. We recognize His love for us right from the start.

Jesus invites us to address God as He does, as Father. But He also desires that we do so in an intimate and private setting. He instructed us, "When you pray, go into your room, close the door and pray to your Father, who is unseen. Then your Father, who sees what is done in secret, will reward you" (Matthew 6:6).

Focusing on what God wants from our time in prayer with Him leads us to a higher quality of time with Him. He wants only what is best for us. Only by praying with His perspective in mind can we accomplish all that prayer has to offer. Not only do we receive help in our work for Him with orphan care, but we grow closer to Him in our personal relationship with Him.

4. From God's perspective, how does looking at our prayer time with God change prayer for you?

5. Read each Scripture passage below and answer the corresponding question.

   2 Chronicles 7:14: What are we to do before we pray?

   Romans 12:12: How are we to be in prayer?

   Ephesians 6:18: When are we to pray?

PRAYING THROUGH THE DAY OF MINISTRY

Often from the very start, I get caught up in my day's list of things to do. Instead, what if I chose God's perspective regarding my list of things to do? Perhaps before I started my day, I could spend time in prayer with Him. My time in prayer could be scattered throughout my day, immediately surrendering all I encountered to Him. My prayers could vary in length—from one sentence prayers to prayers in which I lose all sense of time. Perhaps my to-do list would all be accomplished as He sees fit and to His glory.

Our time in prayer can change us, our parenting, and our ministry.

We tend to use prayer as a last resort, but God wants it to be our first line of defense. We pray when there's nothing else we can do, but God wants us to pray before we do anything at all.

—Oswald Chambers

6. How does John 15:4–5 relate to our prayer life?

7. Reflect on your current prayer time. List any changes in your prayer time God is prompting you to make.

SCRIPTURE MEMORIZATION FOR WEEK 6

Religion that God our Father accepts as pure and faultless is this: to look after orphans and widows in their distress and to keep oneself from being polluted by the world.

—James 1:27

PRAYER

Dear Father, thank You for adopting me and allowing me the undeserved privilege of addressing You as my Father. Create within me the necessary, yielding, and relational aspects of prayer You want me to have. Draw me to You throughout my day. In Jesus' name, amen.

DAY 3

Wrap Around Ministry — Caring for Those Who Care for Others

Those of us who are strong and able in the faith need to step in and lend a hand to those who falter, and not just do what is most convenient for us. Strength is for service, not status. Each one of us needs to look after the good of the people around us, asking ourselves, "How can I help?"

—Romans 15:1–2 *The Message*

We need "Orphan-focused Sundays," but we also need far more—we need orphan-focused churches. Choosing to stand by and do nothing where we see injustice, suffering, and evil is wrong. It is sin. We must take active steps to care for orphans. To do anything less is blatant disobedience.

—Johnny Carr, *Orphan Justice: How to Care for Orphans Beyond Adopting*

CARING FOR THE CAREGIVERS

Dorita and her family began their foster care family ministry in 2009. Over the years, they have fostered or provided long-term respite for ten children.

However, God's call to foster and adopt happened long before 2009. Dorita remembers being called to adoption as early as the 1990s. "I pulled out an article from a Christian magazine on the topic of international adoption," Dorita told me. "I kept it in a box of articles I had collected over the years, and I would pull them out and reread them every now and again."

Then in 2004, Dorita and her husband became acquainted with another family who was also involved with foster care. As they witnessed this other couple's example, Dorita and her husband felt they should also get involved in foster care. It would be through that ministry experience that God would bring them their adopted daughter, Sarah.

Shortly after adopting, Dorita's husband's employers moved them from Texas to Michigan. They immediately connected with a church and got involved. They were overjoyed to discover that their new church had a layperson-led ministry (meaning a member of the congregation started and supplied all the needs for the ministry) for adoptive families called Children of the Heart. It had started in the 1990s—at the same time Dorita first felt God's nudge toward adoption.

Over the decades, it blossomed into a church-supported ministry (a ministry that the church took responsibility for, assigned personnel, and financially contributed toward), called MOSIAC Central and began networking with like-minded churches in the city. Dorita volunteered, and after many years of being involved with the ministry, she became the ministry's coordinator in early 2017.

MOSIAC Central is focused on caring for families who have fostered or adopted. Their work includes:

- Reaching out to new foster care or adoptive families, providing meals, beds, and gift cards, as well as making sure they are aware of agencies that offer support.
- Assisting existing adoptive and foster care families, especially those who are experiencing a rough time, through encouragement cards, making sure the family is aware of others praying for them, and offering personalized support.
- Hosting Mom's Mornings and Nights Out for relaxation and community building.
- Offering a large, indoor play area where foster and adoptive families gather on occasion to encourage and support one another.
- Collecting backpacks with clothing items and toiletries to donate to children new to foster care through a local ministry.
- Facilitating an Orphan Sunday event to recognize all the church families who minister through foster care or adoption, and to introduce others to ways they can be part of this ministry by becoming a foster or adoptive family or supporting those who do.
- Facilitating a community support group.

They have plans to expand the ministry by developing a respite care program (complete with training and background checks), creating needs-specific prayer groups, and offering mentors for foster care and adoptive families.

When a church supports ministering to the vulnerable, the families who foster or adopt feel loved on, ministered to, and encouraged. By caring for the families, the church is caring for the vulnerable. It all starts with someone saying yes—and then encouraging others to join them.

1. What part of Dorita's story and ministry stood out to you? Why?

2. How involved is your church in foster care and adoptive ministry?

3. In what ways could you be the motivational tool God uses to encourage your church's deeper involvement?

4. Read the following Scripture passages and answer how we are encouraged to care.

Proverbs 14:31

Proverbs 19:17

Proverbs 29:7

CARING FOR THOSE JESUS LOVES

We have seen those who quietly minister for God's glory. The humble servants who often appear tired also seem joyful and have a quick smile. A few are employed by the local church and serve as missionaries in a different country or within their own communities. They are also made up of adoptive families, foster care families, and those who work with children at risk, social workers, adoption agencies, and foster care agencies. Their mission is seldom recognized for what it is, a God-honoring ministry. Recognition here on earth is not what they seek. Yet they inspire us.

Those who work in the name of the Lord, particularly among vulnerable children, are seldom encouraged. Their work is often taken for granted, yet their work is daily changing the lives of future generations. They are praying for every child they encounter. Can you imagine how far the slightest encouragement would go among these exhausted workers for Christ?

Throughout the Bible, but especially in Paul's letters to the churches, we find encouragement for such ministry leaders.

Most work in ministry requires sacrifice, and perhaps even suffering. That was the message Paul gave to those in Corinth when he wrote, "Since we have this ministry, just as we received mercy [from God, granting us salvation, opportunities, and blessings], we do not get discouraged nor lose our motivation" (2 Corinthians 4:1 AMP). Christ not only gives us power, but he showers us with love and self-control. God's power through His spirit encourages our striving.

Paul compelled the churches to continue in ministry as an example to others. Ephesians 4:11–13 (CEV) says, "Christ chose some of us to be apostles, prophets, missionaries, pastors, and teachers, so that his people would learn to serve and his body would grow strong. This will continue until we are united by our faith and by our understanding of the Son of God. Then we will be mature, just as Christ is, and we will be completely like him." The body of Christ grows stronger through those who serve. Through testimony, we can share in the miracles that those serving often bear witness to. We are encouraged to keep serving until we are united with Christ.

Paul also encouraged those in ministry to keep high standards. In 2 Corinthians 6:3–4 (CEV) we find, "We don't want anyone to find fault with our work, and so we try hard not to cause problems. But in everything and in every way we show that we truly are God's servants. We have always been patient, though we have had a lot of trouble, suffering, and hard times." In order to continue God's work, we must try to remain as faultless and problem-free as possible, just as Paul tried to be. Fortunately, God works through those in ministry to help them stay focused on Him while serving others. He will complete His work through us (see Philippians 1:6).

Regardless of your ministry, whether it be in another country, your neighborhood, or in your living room, be encouraged in your struggle. Keep in constant contact with the One who sent you to your ministry in the first place. He will never leave you.

5. Which of the verses we've discussed today most apply to your ministry? Why?

6. Read each Scripture passage and answer the corresponding question.

1 Corinthians 10:24: Who are we to look out for?

Philippians 2:4: Whose welfare should we be concerned with?

Hebrews 6:10: How will God reward those who care for other believers?

THE CHURCH AND ORPHAN CARE

The Bible makes God's mandate clear: every Christian must help the orphaned. How we are called to care is the responsibility of each church and member. We must continually evaluate God's mandate for us by asking ourselves:

How am I to help care for the orphaned?
How is our church to care for the orphaned?

One way both the church and the individual members can care for the orphan is to support the members of the congregation who provide direct care. By the church family wrapping around the families who open their hearts and homes to orphaned and vulnerable children, the entire congregation enjoys a front-row seat to the blessings and trials of such intimate care. By supporting their ministries financially, members can play a role in caring for the fatherless.

Such care invites our Father to dwell among us. Such care pays forward care of the vulnerable to future generations. Serving those who care for the orphaned and vulnerable is an incredible way to live out the love of God.

> Since we are in Christ, we have a missionary identity. We are adopted into a missionary family. We serve a missionary God. Mission becomes part of our identity, because our Father is a missionary God and we resemble him as children of God. The church is a missionary church with missionary people who do missionary things for the glory of our missionary God. This is who we *are*, but it is also what we *do*.
>
> —Scott Thomas and Tom Wood, *Gospel Coach: Shepherding Leaders to Glorify God*

7. How have you been called to ministry in your living room, in your community, or in the world?

8. Describe what that ministry looks like and why you feel called to it.

SCRIPTURE MEMORIZATION FOR WEEK 6

Religion that God our Father accepts as pure and faultless is this: to look after orphans and widows in their distress and to keep oneself from being polluted by the world.

—James 1:27

PRAYER

Dear Father, You are a mission-oriented God, and I thank and praise You for it. Thank You for sending Your son, Jesus Christ. Thank You for sending Your church out to a hurting world. Embolden us. Reside with us. Teach us what to say. May our hands be Your hands. In Jesus' name, amen.

DAY 4

From Mission Trip to International Ministry

Go and make disciples of all nations, baptizing them in the name of the Father and of the Son and of the Holy Spirit, and teaching them to obey everything I have commanded you. And surely I am with you always, to the very end of the age.

—Matthew 28:19–20

There's a day that is coming when all the last will be first and every orphan will be home.

—Steven Curtis Chapman, "A Little More Time to Love"

THERE IS NOTHING HE CANNOT DO

God certainly works in different and mysterious ways. Some He calls to adoption. Some He calls to both adoption inside the home and a ministry outside the home. Some He calls to that work by way of a magazine article or a book. Some He calls through a mission trip, just as he did Beth and Todd Guckenberger.

Beth and Todd were teachers, and they spent their summers taking youth from their church on mission trips. In 1996, during a mission trip to Mexico in which they were painting buildings, Beth felt as though the work they were doing wasn't making much difference. "I complained to my husband, who was painting beside me," Beth said. "He asked me if I thought there were any orphanages nearby."

Years before this trip to Mexico, Todd and Beth had been on another mission trip together in Albania. Beth knew why Todd was asking about an orphanage. The work they performed at an orphanage there had been the highlight of their trip.

They jumped in a taxi, and after explaining in their limited Spanish where they wanted the cab driver to take them, they ended up at an orphanage. Through some creative communication, the driver helped them translate, and they asked the director if the orphanage needed any work done. "We explained that we had twenty-five young people, $200, and one day remaining on our trip," Beth said. "The director pointed out a broken window and mentioned that the children had not eaten meat for the last year." They returned the next day, fixed the window, bought and prepared meat for the children, "and our hearts were broken for the vulnerable."

Through that experience, Beth and Todd followed God's leading and prepared for a year's work in Monterrey, Mexico. They lived on only one of their two salaries and managed to save $25,000 and prepared to take a one-year leave from their teaching jobs. That was more than twenty years ago, the beginning of Back2Back Ministries, and they are still serving.

"God has an incredible way of drawing His people into care for the vulnerable," Beth said. That first year, they invited fifty people from their home church to visit Monterrey and witness their work helping orphans, and throughout the course of that year, more than 350 showed up. "Once they saw God at work there, they started giving to His work," Beth said. "Once they started giving, they started doing work for Him. It's a beautiful cycle."

Today, Back2Back works in six countries—the Dominican Republic, Haiti, India, Mexico, Nigeria, and the United States—and has an annual operating budget of more than $10 million.

"Our kids have grown up in the ministry," Beth told me. "They've traveled the world. They've shared their holidays with others. My mama's heart wants to minimize the cost of ministry and maximize the benefit, but we all know that is not always possible."

When asked how the years of ministry to the vulnerable has affected her faith, Beth sighed with contentment. "I knew God worked in miraculous ways, but I had never asked Him to. Now I've watched Him accomplish the impossible. I've watched Him just be Himself. There is nothing He cannot do. It's pretty phenomenal."

> I don't ever have to wonder if I've asked God too many times or for too much. I can just ask Him to be God.
>
> —Beth Guckenberger

1. Which part of Beth's story encourages you the most? Why?

2. How does Beth's story inspire you regarding prayer?

3. Read the following Scripture passages and answer how God calls us to reach others with our faith.

   1 Chronicles 16:24

   Psalm 96:3

   Acts 13:47

REVEALING THE GOOD NEWS BY CARING FOR THE ORPHAN

Whether serving in our own country or serving abroad, serving the orphaned and vulnerable is a wonderful opportunity to live out the gospel. We can display it to those we serve, those who watch us serve, and to one another.

To do those things well, we must develop a servant's heart, something Micah 6:8 explains how to do: "He has shown you, O mortal, what is good. And what does the LORD require of you? To act justly and to love mercy and to walk humbly with your God."

Micah reminds us that our service to others is the good news made visible and in action. We see that most clearly in three ways.

By acting justly.
To act justly means we know what is right and wrong, and we do what is right. We know our Father's heart for the orphaned, and He wants us to care for them, in whatever way He calls us. In Isaiah 1:17 (ESV), that calling includes bringing justice for the orphan: "Learn to do good; seek justice, correct oppression; bring justice to the fatherless, plead the widow's cause." By acting justly on behalf of the orphaned, we are able to be an example to others of God's love for them also.

By loving mercy.
To truly have mercy on someone is to show them compassion, especially outside the limits of what the world deems as normal. Showing such mercy or compassion for those so vulnerable begs the question *why*. God sees their trouble and has compassion for the orphan, as it says in Psalm 10:14 (CEV): "You see the trouble and the distress, and you will do something. The poor can count on you, and so can orphans." By showing mercy to those for whom the world does not, we give glory to God.

By walking humbly.
To walk humbly with God is to walk sacrificially among those He loves. In Acts 20:35 (ESV), Paul reminds us of Jesus' words about the blessing of sacrifice, "In all things I have shown you that by working hard in this way we must help the weak and remember the words of the Lord Jesus, how he himself said, 'It is more blessed to give than to receive.'" By humbly following God and serving the orphaned, we are sacrificing whatever we give up so that they may gain love and family and acceptance—to their blessing and ours.

The good news of the gospel through the sacrifice of Jesus' life, in order that we become children of God, is the very image of God we imitate in orphan care. Any sacrifice we make is to thank Him for what He has done for us. Imitating Christ's sacrifice by exchanging the sacrifice of our lives for the life of an orphan is weak by comparison, yet it is one we make to the glory of God.

4. How is the good news displayed through orphan care?

5. Read each Scripture passage and answer the corresponding question.

Mark 16:15: We are to go into the world and do what?

John 1:12: Who has the right to become the children of God?

Romans 10:15: How beautiful are the feet that do what?

A FAMILY RECONCILED

The Island of Hope Center in Yuzhny, Ukraine, provides vulnerable children afterschool, medical, and nutrition care in addition to entertainment and relaxation services, humanitarian aid to vulnerable families, and social visitations. The chief coordinator, Stepan Koisa, and his wife Lina oversee the seven-days-a-week operation. Recently, a young girl started visiting the center. Her parents had divorced, and she was acting out at home and school. Even though she was new to the center, she was invited to attend Bible camp. She didn't want to go, but the center staff and her mother encouraged her to attend.

After only one day of camp, the staff noticed a difference in the young girl. She wanted to learn as much about God and His Word as she could. That change in her continued when she returned home, and even her mother noticed a difference.

Her mother was so impressed that she went to the church where the center is located. After attending services for three weeks, her mother became saved. But God didn't stop there.

The mother and daughter were so changed, the ex-husband and father began questioning them. He was unsure of their church affiliation, so he made a complaint with the local prosecutor's office, asking them to investigate. When they refused, he followed the girl and her mother to the church. Weeks later, he too came to know the Lord. The family has been reconciled.

This is just another way God works through those reaching out to the vulnerable. When the ministry becomes challenging, God encourages our hearts through such amazing works of His grace and the lives changed by it.

The knowledge that the Father has bestowed his love on us, so that we are called children of God—and in fact are his children (1 John 3:1–2)—will, over time, prove to be the solvent in which our fears, mistrust, and suspicion of God—as well as our sense of distance from him—will eventually dissolve.

—Sinclair B. Ferguson, *Children of the Living God*

6. According to 1 John 3:1–2, why does the world not know, or recognize, us as His children?

7. Reflect on how caring for the orphaned and vulnerable helps spread the gospel. List those ways and star the ones you most connect with.

SCRIPTURE MEMORIZATION FOR WEEK 6

Religion that God our Father accepts as pure and faultless is this: to look after orphans and widows in their distress and to keep oneself from being polluted by the world.

—James 1:27

PRAYER

Dear Father, thank You for not only calling me to Your holy work but also for allowing me to be Your hands and feet to others. Encourage my heart to love as You love. Comfort my disappointments. Inspire me to reach beyond the humanly possible. In Jesus' name, amen.

DAY 5

Imagining a World with No More Orphans

In Christ Jesus you are all children of God through faith, for all of you who were baptized into Christ have clothed yourselves with Christ. There is neither Jew nor Gentile, neither slave nor free, nor is there male and female, for you are all one in Christ Jesus. If you belong to Christ, then you are Abraham's seed, and heirs according to the promise.

—Galatians 3:26–29

If the gospel is ultimately the story of those who were empty and orphaned from God being adopted into His family by the work of Jesus, then our care for and adoption of vulnerable, neglected, abused, marginalized, and orphaned children is a beautiful continuation of the redemption story of God and a vivid demonstration of the love of Jesus extended through us.

—Jason Johnson, "3 Reasons Why the Church Must Care for Orphans," *Jason Johnson* blog

ADOPTION IS NOT CHARITY

Steve Weber remembers the night in the fall of 2008 when a few godly men met in his living room to pray. It was there his friend Nikolay Kuleba (currently serving with Ombudsman for Children with the president of Ukraine) prayed, "I want to live in a Ukraine without orphans." Steve and everyone in the room was struck by Nikolay's prayer. That one sentence planted the seed within the group to begin a movement for Ukraine Without Orphans, which eventually catalyzed as World Without Orphans (WWO).

Today, WWO is a shared vision in more than forty countries and is made up of more than 150 individuals, churches, and nongovernmental organizations (NGOs). Through WWO, members work to understand and educate others regarding the total scope of the global orphan crisis with a goal of developing the best possible solutions.

"What I've come to understand is that adoption is not charity, but spiritual warfare," Steve told me. "To redeem the orphan from the culture of orphanhood is relatively easy, compared to rescuing the child from what we call the orphan spirit. That's the battle."

The orphan spirit is best explained the way it is formed. A child is institutionalized, for whatever reason. Their questions are: *When will I be cared for? When will I have a mother and a father? When will I have a home?* But their *when* never comes.

That's when a new script begins. They start to believe, *I'm wrong. I'm not pretty enough. I'm not the right gender, the right size. I don't have the right hair or skin color.*

That internal script leads to the orphan spirit that believes, *I'm on my own. I have to be a survivor. I don't need parents or a home. I am an orphan. I don't need anyone.*

This is what the WWO teams are fighting against. It is a real and often ugly spiritual battle. They are working toward restoring the orphan's self-worth through placement in family and other forms of nurturing care.

"God said He is the father of the fatherless, which means He wants every orphan to be in a family," Ruslan Maliuta, leader of the WWO, said. "How is God going to do it? It's through the church. Adoption and providing a home for an orphan is an integral part of the gospel."

Advocates from around the world are making a difference, here on earth and for eternity, and all for the glory of God. We are all to play a part in orphan care. Only God can answer what role He specifically wants each of us to play.

Asking God what our role is may be the most intimidating part of orphan care. The Apostle James gives us further instructions: "If you don't know what you're doing, pray to the Father. He loves to help. You'll get his help, and won't be condescended to when you ask for it. Ask boldly, believingly, without a second thought. People who 'worry their prayers' are like wind-whipped waves. Don't think you're going to get anything from the Master that way, adrift at sea, keeping all your options open" (James 1:5–8 *The Message*). God longs to guide your steps.

1. How has adoption changed your view of your relationship with God?

2. What other ways has adoption or orphan care influenced your faith?

3. Take a few moments and imagine a world without orphans, in which every child has a family, is nurtured, and is loved. Describe that world.

4. Read the following Scripture passages and answer how we have the right to be called children of God.

   Romans 8:14

Galatians 3:26

Ephesians 1:5

THE SPIRITUAL BLESSING OF ADOPTION

Adoption is an integral part of orphan care. It becomes the main focus when family reconciliation fails. Institutions and foster care cannot replace the stability adoption offers. Adoption can be a blessing for all involved.

Our spiritual adoption has special blessings for believers also:

I am special to God.
First Peter 2:9–10 says, "You are a chosen people, a royal priesthood, a holy nation, God's special possession, that you may declare the praises of him who called you out of darkness into his wonderful light. Once you were not a people, but now you are the people of God; once you had not received mercy, but now you have received mercy." As God's adopted children, we bear witness to once having been lost and now found. We knew what it was to be orphaned and now adopted. We know what it is to receive His undeserved grace. Our lives are to declare that message to the world.

I can cry out to Him.
We "fear not," for we know the God of the universe in a relational way. We have only to cry out to Him. He has our best interests at heart, as most fathers would. In Romans 8:14–15, Paul wrote, "For those who are led by the Spirit of God are the children of God. The Spirit you received does not make you slaves, so that you live in fear again; rather, the Spirit you received brought about your adoption to sonship. And by him we cry, 'Abba, Father.'" As His adopted children, He will hear our cry.

I am not alone.
God always knew we could not be holy on our own. He had to rescue us from our sinful nature. He made the ultimate sacrifice of allowing His only Son to die for us. Then He sent the Holy Spirit to reside in us. In John 14:16–18, Jesus said, "I will ask the Father, and he will give you another advocate to help you and be with you forever—the Spirit of truth. The world cannot

accept him, because it neither sees him nor knows him. But you know him, for he lives with you and will be in you. I will not leave you as orphans; I will come to you." God has not left us alone. His spirit is such a gracious present. A value beyond our imagination. Such a humbling, undeserved gift.

These are the gifts only those who have been adopted into God's family can understand. We have been blessed by our adoption, and our lives and our world will never be the same.

5. Which spiritual blessing of adoption draws you most to God? Why?

6. Read each Scripture passage and answer the corresponding question.

Romans 8:15: We enjoy the Spirit of God because of what?

Ephesians 5:1: As children of God, how are we to be?

1 John 3:1: How do we get to relate to God?

A CALL TO ACTION

The same adoption that can bring such encouragement and joy can also bring pain and disappointment. Svetlana's death was a blow to our family. From the United States, through friends in ministry in Ukraine, I helped arrange her burial. They held a short graveside service for her in Odessa. We had a small memorial service for her at our church in Michigan.

In memory of Svetlana, and with the assistance of godly brothers and sisters in the region, we started a nonprofit ministry called Nourished Hearts, which ministers to the orphaned in the Odessa Oblast area of Ukraine. Though small, the work we are doing is mighty. Stepan Koisa, an elder of Bethel Baptist Church in Yuzhny, Ukraine, and a social worker by trade, along with his staff and volunteers, have developed a relationship with a government-run orphanage to provide life-assistance classes, spiritual classes, and to host children from the orphanage who have nowhere to go during holidays and breaks.

They also operate the Island of Hope Center in Yuzhny, Ukraine. Open seven days a week, this center enables vulnerable families to receive care for their children so they can work outside of the home. The children receive tutoring, snacks, and meals, meet with social workers and medical professionals, and enjoy Bible stories and crafts.

They are in process of establishing a mentoring program to those young people who have aged out of the orphanage system. Stepan and his group could use your prayer support.

After all that has been covered in this study, consider this your call to take action. In some way, you are called to care for the orphaned, vulnerable, and marginalized—perhaps beyond your personal experience with adoption or foster care. Perhaps by furthering your adoption and foster care experience. Perhaps by encouraging others to adopt. Perhaps it is through another area of orphan care that you aren't even yet aware of. Ask for the Spirit's guidance. Pray specifically and intentionally. God has so much in store for you.

Yes, a child's life could be drastically changed by God's leading in your life. But perhaps there is another person God longs to love, change, and embrace. And it's you.

> The truth is that the 143 million orphaned children and the 11 million who starve to death or die from preventable diseases and the 8.5 million who work as child slaves, prostitutes, or under other horrific conditions and the 2.3 million who live with HIV add up to 164.8 million needy children. And though at first glance that looks like a big number, 2.1 billion people on this earth proclaim to be Christians. The truth is that if only 8 percent of the Christians would care for one more child, there would not be any statistics left.
>
> —Katie J. Davis, *Kisses from Katie: A Story of Relentless Love and Redemption*

7. According to Philippians 1:9–11, what does God want regarding our love for others?

8. Reflect on the ways in which helping the orphaned (or considering it) has deepened your faith. Write those down and put them into a prayer, thanking God for how He leads you and asking Him for His continued guidance as you work to be obedient to His call.

SCRIPTURE MEMORIZATION FOR WEEK 6

Religion that God our Father accepts as pure and faultless is this: to look after orphans and widows in their distress and to keep oneself from being polluted by the world.

—James 1:27

PRAYER

Dear Father, thank You for Your love. Thank You for redeeming me. Thank You for the way You have provided us to become members of Your family—through adoption. Thank You for allowing me to care for others. Remind me always that my actions are to give all praise and glory to You. In Jesus' name, amen.

Acknowledgments

It is a bit intimidating to finish the long journey of a book, only then to try and thank all of those who played a part along the way. It is my prayer all have been mentioned. There are simply so many people to thank.

First and foremost, to my heavenly, adoptive Father, without whom I could not have written a word. You faithfully met me at my laptop, just as I asked.

To my husband Jahn. Your sacrifice and support for my writing, speaking, and ministry only speaks to the Christlikeness I see in you daily. It is so great that I get to spend my days with you.

To our daughter Jacey. Your beauty is matched only by your heart for all things animal. Your support has meant so much to me personally. You are my favorite girl in the world.

To our son Jake. You have brought so much joy to our family and to my heart. You are a special young man. I am proud of you.

To my parents, Judy, Rodney, Ann, Jim, Jacob, and Charlotte. Your daily support and memories bring me joy and comfort. You continue to parent me as an adult. I have been blessed by having you in my life.

To my extended family and friends. Your support during the writing of this book (and beyond) has not gone unnoticed. I thank God for you.

To my agent Steve Laube. We both know this book would not have happened without your support, knowledge, and connections. God has used you in my life. I am grateful.

To my personal editor and friend, Ginger Kolbaba. You know my voice as well as I do. I continue to learn from you. You are a gift from God, my friend.

To my new friends at New Hope Publishing, including Ramona Richards, Tina Atchenson, Meredith Dunn, and Reagan Jackson. Your support was crucial in this publishing journey. God uses you in mighty ways, my friends.

To my church micro group—Becky, Jen, Karen, and Laura. Your prayers encouraged much more than you know.

To the ministry team of Nourished Hearts, in the US and in Ukraine. It is an honor to work beside you, Karen, Ron, Lisa, Loralyn, Alex, Andrea, Jahn, and Stepan.

To the many orphan care ministries and adoption agencies located in West Michigan and beyond. Your presence and love for God shines brightly.

To the Word Weavers of West Michigan. The way you embrace writers at all levels is amazing. God works through your acceptance and love. Kathy Bruins, your friendship is something I treasure. Eva Marie Everson, your international leadership is inspiring.

To the conferences I attend regularly—the Christian Alliance for Orphans, Together for Adoption, Florida Christian Writers Conference, the Advanced Writers and Speakers Association, the Speak Up Conference, and The Well. Thank you for all you have taught and will, no doubt, continue to teach me.

To the countless adoptive parents and orphan care ministry leaders who in some way contributed to this book. May God continue to use you in the lives of others. I see Him in you. You inspire me.

About the Author

Kim de Blecourt loves God, reading His Word, and caring for the vulnerable. With more than a decade of serving in adoption and orphan care ministries, Kim is passionate about God's people embracing the orphaned.

Kim serves as the founder and president of Nourished Hearts (Holland, Michigan), an international orphan care nonprofit. She previously worked with Food for Orphans (Colorado Springs, Colorado) and has volunteered in promoting adoption and vulnerable childcare in Washington, DC. She has participated in legislation preparation and grass roots efforts for changes in international child welfare and the human rights of children to be in families.

A recipient of *Focus on Women* magazine's Quill Award as a Resilient Woman, Kim is also the author of *Until We All Come Home: A Harrowing Journey, a Mother's Courage, a Race to Freedom*.

A popular speaker regarding orphan care, Kim is a member of the Speak Up speaker team and serves as an author mentor at the Speak Up Conference. She teaches at the Florida Christian Writers Conference and is a member of the Advanced Writers and Speakers Association, a member of the Christian Alliance for Orphans, and a past presenter at the Together for Adoption Conference.

Kim lives in Michigan with her husband and children. When she's not writing or speaking, you will find her walking their dog or singing on the worship team at her home church.

Website
kimdeblecourt.com

Twitter
twitter.com/kimdeblecourtauthor

Ministry
nourishedhearts.org

Pinterest
pinterest.com
/kimdeblecourtauthor

Speaking
kimdeblecourt@gmail.com

Facebook
facebook.com
/kimdeblecourtauthor

The Christian Alliance for Orphans (CAFO)

CAFO serves as a hub for the global movement of Christians committed to adoption, foster care, and orphan ministry.

Through CAFO, some 190 respected organizations and a worldwide network of churches work together to equip God's people for wise, effective action. CAFO offers a wide array of excellent videos, podcasts, booklets, handouts, and other resources—most at no cost.

CAFO initiatives connect and serve foster and adoptive parents, pastors, and lay leaders of church ministries, nonprofits that desire to continue improving their programs, donors seeking to maximize the impact of their giving, students looking to learn and serve, and more.

Each May, the CAFO Summit draws this community together from around the world to learn and grow side-by-side. Each November, Orphan Sunday—now celebrated in more than ninety countries—provides an opportunity for individuals and churches to spread God's heart for orphans and foster youth.

If you desire to live out God's deep love for orphaned and vulnerable children wisely and well, learn more at www.CAFO.org.

CAFO
Christian Alliance for Orphans

If you enjoyed this book, will you consider sharing the message with others?

Let us know your thoughts at info@newhopepublishers.com. You can also let the author know by visiting or sharing a photo of the cover on our social media pages or leaving a review at a retailer's site. All of it helps us get the message out!

Twitter.com/NewHopeBooks

Facebook.com/NewHopePublishers

Instagram.com/NewHopePublishers

———————

New Hope® Publishers is an imprint of Iron Stream Media, which derives its name from Proverbs 27:17, "As iron sharpens iron, so one person sharpens another."

This sharpening describes the process of discipleship, one to another. With this in mind, Iron Stream Media provides a variety of solutions for churches, missionaries, and nonprofits ranging from in-depth Bible study curriculum and Christian book publishing to custom publishing and consultative services. Through the popular Life Bible Study and Student Life Bible Study brands, ISM provides web-based full-year and short-term Bible study teaching plans as well as printed devotionals, Bibles, and discipleship curriculum.

For more information on ISM and New Hope Publishers, please visit

IronStreamMedia.com

NewHopePublishers.com